Shining Through the Grief
Memoirs of Emma's Mom

Meredith D. Duke

Copyright © 2013 by Meredith Duke

All Rights Reserved.

ISBN-10: 0989084604

ISBN-13: 978-0-9890846-0-4

Edited by Artie Stockton

Scripture taken from the New King James Version®. Copyright © 1983 by Thomas Nelson, Inc. Used by permission. All rights reserved.

Dedication

This book is dedicated to my Heavenly Father. Without Him we would not have been blessed with beautiful Emma, our miracle baby.

I also dedicate this book to our sweet Emma Danielle. Jesus rocks her for me until I can hold her again.

To God goes the glory.

Emma

Beautiful Emma - so pretty and sweet,
In heaven we shall meet.

We held you for a moment, an angel so dear,
It was the moment our lives became so clear.

You touched our hearts and made them melt,
Our tears of joy I hope you felt.

Jesus rocks you now in heaven,
But one day we shall be together.

Beautiful Emma - so pretty and sweet,
We count the days before we meet.

Table of Contents

The Silent Prayer 1

Sweet Emma 5

Walking on the Water with Jesus 25

Emma's Journal, Eulogy & Message 31

God's Plan for You 53

Lessons Learned 59

Shine On 69

A Dad's Perspective 75

Epilogue 77

Acknowledgments

I thank God for every blessing in my life. Without Him I would be nothing but through Him I am one of His children, an heir to His heavenly kingdom. Through His love and grace I will see my beautiful baby girl again one day in heaven. My mantra over the years has been, "I can do all things through Christ who strengthens me" (Philippians 4:13). This quote really kept me going in the months after Emma's death. Even now I try to keep this in mind throughout all of my trials, tribulations and joys. God deserves the glory, not me or my family. It is by God's grace and mercy that we have been able to mourn Emma and heal at the same time. He gave me the strength to write this book and re-live those sad and painful times surrounding Emma's birth and death.

Thank you to my sweet husband, Johnny. The Lord has certainly blessed me with a wonderful, loving, God-fearing husband. Little did we know as a young married couple that one day we would endure the death of our baby. We suffered much through losing Emma and we still mourn a little every day, but together with God's strength and love we have overcome the toughest situation that any parents should have to face. I love Johnny more than he will ever know. He was a rock of faith, love, patience, kindness, all that a husband could be in such a difficult situation. I thank the Lord every day for Johnny. When the tears fell and words could not comfort, it were his arms that held me and loved me.

My children, James and Lauren, are the epitome of goodness in this world. James was the young man of the house when Johnny was at work. When I was pregnant, he kept me from falling several times, carried items for me, and generally pitched in with whatever was asked of him. Following Emma's death, Lauren has been a quiet consoler, giving hugs and kisses or holding my hand at just the right moment. The Lord truly blessed our family with these two precious children. I love them so dearly and consider them to be my biggest blessings in life.

To my sister, Charlsye Szymanski, and my brother-in-law, Chris Szymanski, thank you for sitting with us in the hospital all day, for just being there with us. Thank you to my in-laws, Joe and Betty Duke, for watching over James and Lauren while we were in the hospital. Also, thank you for donating Emma's burial plot. It means so much to us knowing that she is buried next to her great-grandmother. To my dad, Charlie Dalley and my stepmom, Linda Dalley, thank you for rushing to the hospital when I needed you the most. To my mom, Ursula Dalley, thank you for crocheting Emma's precious pink blanket.

To the staff of the Austin Area Birthing Center, what can I say? You were there with me during my entire pregnancy. Charlotte and Samantha, you were with us during delivery and held our hands, prayed with us and consoled us when we found out Emma was going to be stillborn. You cried and mourned with us. Mary and Roswitha called and spoke with me about their own losses. Tamara, your smiling face and "Hey, girl!" will always be with us. You will never know how much we truly appreciate you all. We consider you part of our extended family and love you very much. Thank you for all that you do for first-time mothers and even us veterans who have been through childbirth before. You are strong, courageous women who step into the chaos of a delivery and bring experience, serenity, wisdom and love to an emotionally charged, physically demanding situation. God bless you. You do this world a fantastic service and are such a joy to those who know you.

I also want to give a huge thank you to Dionne Hiebert, a volunteer photographer with the nonprofit group, Now I Lay Me Down to Sleep (NILMDTS). Dionne came to the hospital and photographed our beautiful daughter. She was gentle with Emma and patient and compassionate with Johnny and me. All of the photographs that Dionne took of Emma are labeled with her name. She did such a marvelous job and truly captured the beauty of Emma and our love for her.

If you are not familiar with NILMDTS, it is a non-profit organization that blesses parents with a free photography session in the hospital (or other hospice location) so when parents leave the hospital without their precious baby they have a way to remember their child for years to come. Our portraits of Emma are beautiful and touching. I thank God for this wonderful organization and the service they provided to not only us but to other grieving parents as well.

To all our friends and family who showed up at the hospital, sent messages and emails or simply called to check on us, thank you for your support, prayers and love. You truly helped us through those first few weeks. We felt blessed to be loved by all of you and could literally feel the love and prayers pour over us during this journey in our lives.

Thank you to the one who paid for Emma's funeral. We know who you are and while you have asked to remain anonymous, we humbly thank you for your generosity and love. It was a gesture that will always be remembered and treasured.

Introduction

Losing a child is one of the most painful experiences a parent can endure. I never thought this would happen to our family. I always believed that something this tragic happened "to other people," not us. At least that is what I thought until we lost our baby, Emma Danielle.

My hope is that through this book you will understand that various parts of this book can apply to many situations: loss of a child, parent, sibling or other loved one; divorce, substance abuse, marital issues, financial situations, or whatever else you may be facing. Yes, it is about the death of a newborn, but more than that, it is a book on how to lean on Jesus and trust in Him through whatever battle may be raging in or around you. It is about how we can let God's light shine through us in our deepest misery and sorrow so that others may come to know Jesus and accept Him as their Lord and Savior. Johnny and I have really taken to heart what King David wrote in Psalm 27:1, "The Lord is my light and my salvation."

Jesus said that the two greatest commandments are to love the Lord with all your heart, soul and mind and secondly, to love our neighbors as ourselves (Matthew 22:37-39). Here is how I can show my love for you: by revealing to you what we did in our unbelievably difficult situation in the hope that you will be able to benefit from it and apply it to your life and whatever battles you may be facing.

May God bless each one of you as you read this book, and may God's love shine on you so that in turn you may be a light and blessing to others in their time of need.

In HIS Love,
Meredith Duke
www.shineonbook.weebly.com

Part I

Our Story

Chapter 1
The Silent Prayer

Be anxious for nothing, but in everything by prayer and supplication, with thanksgiving, let your requests be made known to God. - Philippians 4:6

Have you ever had a silent prayer? You know - the one private prayer that you have been hoping and praying would come true. The one that God would answer, "Yes." My silent prayer was to have another child. I lifted that prayer to God every week for many years, hoping and praying that He would say, "Yes."

God had already blessed us with two beautiful children, James and Lauren. We also have an angel in heaven from a miscarriage I had in 1997. James is our oldest. He is our thinker and planner, the entrepreneur of our family. Our daughter Lauren is the free spirit in our family, the effervescent bubble that never pops.

After all the years of waiting and hoping for another child, I figured that God's answer was "no." After all, Lauren was eight years old at that time and I was approaching forty. Although I still had a hope that maybe, just maybe, God would change His mind, I was okay with His answer.

Even though my silent prayer was to have another child, my husband, Johnny, had often stated that he did not think we should have any more children. Early in our marriage (within the first year we were married and long before we had James), Johnny had a dream of two young blond children (a boy and a girl) standing at the end of a table. He knew in his heart that these were the children we would have some day. So, any time we talked about additional children, he would remind me of his dream and say that he believed God just intended for us to have two.

For several years we had been following the Dave Ramsey plan and by June 2010, we were finally debt free and reaping the benefits of a debt-free life: planning lots of vacations, starting to build our six-month emergency fund, saving for our own land, etc. In our minds we were well on our way to the next stage of our lives – financial freedom. We had lived like no one else so that now we could live like no one else (you know what that means if you follow Dave Ramsey's Financial Peace plan). But, God had other plans for us.

By July 2010 (one month later), I was late. That was somewhat normal as my cycle for the previous few months had been sporadic. I thought I was pre-menopausal. After being late for too many days, I thought we should rule out pregnancy before I made an appointment with a doctor. I was not really worried yet, just being logical. After all, what would a doctor do first? Rule out pregnancy. I figured I would start with the obvious and then go from there. It was Sunday, July 4th and after church we went by the local grocery store and I purchased a pregnancy test. Johnny thought I was crazy but I told him, "It's just to rule it out." I took the first of the two tests in the package, fully expecting a negative result. However, to my utter and complete astonishment it was positive! I remember sitting down on the side of the bathtub, just taking it in, absorbing the news and wondering how to tell Johnny. A positive result was not what I expected (what I had hoped and prayed for, but not what I expected after all the years of praying).

When Johnny came in from outside, I still had not stepped out of the bathroom. He asked through the door, "It's negative?"

"No," I replied.

"You're not pregnant, right?"

"No," I said.

After a long pause on the other side of the door I heard, "Wait ... it's positive?"

"Yes," I simply replied.

I opened the door and Johnny was just standing there, with his mouth hanging down to the floor in shock. Slowly he turned towards me with a glazed look in his eyes. I do not think he even really saw me. He gave me this half-hearted hug and said, "Congratulations!" However, I don't think he really meant it at the time. He looked like he had just swallowed a very large pill and was silently choking on it.

Just to confirm the results I took the second test. Yep, it was still positive. That little second line showed up almost immediately.

If you ever think that you are in control, guess again. God is in control. If you think otherwise, it is time to re-evaluate.

Abraham and Sarah had Isaac when they were well past childbearing age[1]. Sarah was in her nineties, so you can imagine why Abraham laughed when God told him Sarah would have a son and they were to name him Isaac (which means laughter). Even Rachel was an older woman when God opened up her womb for her sons, Joseph and Benjamin. I wasn't quite ninety, but I certainly thought God had answered "no," just like these women. That's a good lesson to remember. It doesn't matter what you think God's answer is. He may just surprise you with "yes" when you think the answer is "no."

As we started telling family and friends, we received mixed responses. Some were ecstatic while others were more concerned and shocked than anything else. We heard, "You know how that happens, right?" Or, "Aren't you a little old now?" Okay. I was 37, not exactly old, but not as young as I once was. I believe someone said I was no spring chicken (actually I think that was Johnny). It seemed to be the first thing people thought, *why on earth would you want another child? Your children are already eleven and eight. What are you thinking?!* Truth be told, I was somewhat nervous and those thoughts did enter my mind, but only for a fleeting second. I had wanted this child for so long that I still couldn't believe God had answered "yes" to my silent prayer. I was more excited than anything else. I felt truly blessed and loved by God. What else could I feel? Johnny eventually got to my level of excitement, although it took him a little bit longer. He was pretty much in shock for about two to three weeks (maybe even longer than that).

A few nights after our July 4th announcement, I walked into the living room and saw Johnny staring at the dark, blank TV with his eyes bugged out and his mouth hanging open (actually he looked catatonic). I looked from Johnny to the TV and back to him. "What are you doing?" I asked, somewhat confused.

"Reliving the moment," he said. It still hadn't completely sunk in that we were going to have another baby.

Over the next eight months, we prepared for our little baby. We found out she was going to be a girl (much to James' dismay and Lauren's delight). After much family debate we chose her name, Emma Danielle Duke. In our little home, we started making room for Emma. We rearranged the upstairs to fit Emma's bed (the same bed James and Lauren used). We pulled out all of Lauren's old baby

---

[1] Genesis 17:17.

clothes and washed and folded them for Emma. Lauren helped me register at Target and we attended a couple of baby showers.

In the meantime, there were several other family and friends who were also due around the same time I was. Two of my cousins delivered their babies in February. I was due in March. A co-worker of mine, Crystal, was due in early April. Another cousin was also due in April and my niece was due with her son in late May. Crystal and I would exchange our pregnancy dilemmas, share sonogram photos of our daughters, check in with each other on how we were feeling, etc. It was a truly wonderful time. I enjoyed seeing how my family and friends were doing in their pregnancies and felt so honored to be a part of it as well.

Aside from the daily icky feelings of morning sickness in the first trimester, I enjoyed my pregnancy. I loved to feel Emma kick or "bounce" when she got the hiccups. I looked forward with much excitement to my appointments with the midwives at the birthing center. My heart swelled with joy each time I heard Emma's heartbeat, a sure reminder of the life growing inside me.

As most mothers-to-be know, there is an instant connection between a woman and the baby growing inside her. For me a protective, nurturing instinct kicked in from the moment I first found out I was pregnant. I treasured that connection with Emma as it was such a special time for us. We were able to bond before she was ever born.

Being a mother is one of the absolute joys in my life, from the early days of midnight feedings to the current moments of homeschooling. Every moment is to be cherished, from the daily monotonous chores to the exciting vacations and favorite holiday traditions. I love watching my children grow and learn about God's world.

I simply knew that this baby was a miracle and I loved her from the first day I knew I was carrying her. She was my baby, a gift from God because He loved me and knew what was in my heart. He had answered my silent prayer.

Chapter 2
Sweet Emma

To everything there is a season, a time for every purpose under heaven: a time to be born, and a time to die; a time to weep, and a time to laugh; a time to mourn, and a time to dance; - Ecclesiastes 3: 1-2, 4

The Week of Emma's Due Date

Johnny had taken time off work that week to stay by my side for when I went into labor. There were a few times over the previous week that we thought I was going into labor and he did not want to take any chances. We thought Emma would arrive early since James was seven days early and Lauren was ten days early. At that time, we were down to one vehicle and if he was at work, it would be forty-five minutes before he got home and another forty-five minutes before we made it to the birthing center. It was not a risk we were willing to take. My birthing plan did not include delivering Emma on the side of the highway. After all, a third child can come very quickly! We were thus tied at the hip for the week of Emma's due date. I felt like a queen being chauffeured everywhere I needed to go: the birthing center, grocery store, dairy, and church. It was wonderful. I was pampered and absolutely loving it.

I had tried several things to go into labor all week: baking, walking, gardening, etc. Nothing worked. In the hope that it would entice Emma, I baked a pre-birthday lemon bundt cake (okay – so it was a bribe). I kept telling her, "Come on, Emma, come on out! I made you your first birthday cake!" But, it did not work.

Thursday, March 10th – Countdown to Labor

Emma kicked all the time. She was a very active baby. I often thought she was running a mini marathon in my womb. The last time I felt Emma kick was bedtime on Wednesday night, March 9th.

Thursday morning, March 10th, was pretty normal for us. We woke up, dressed and ate breakfast. James and Lauren started on their school work. Johnny and I spent some time outside. A little before lunchtime, I was watching him do some gardening while I sat on the deck. I had not felt Emma move once that entire morning and mentioned it to Johnny. He thought she might be sleeping. All day I tried different things to see if I could feel her move: drinking coke, eating chocolate, pushing on my belly, plus anything else I could think of, but I did not feel her move one time. It was an eerie feeling since she had always been so active.

That evening around 8 p.m. the labor pains started again. This time it was not just Braxton Hicks contractions. These were real contractions and they were getting closer together and stronger. After a call to the midwife around one o'clock in the morning we decided I should go to the birthing center to see how things were progressing. We loaded up James and Lauren, grabbed the bags of food, Emma's birthday cake (to celebrate her arrival), a few miscellaneous items and headed down into Austin to the birthing center.

Even that early in the morning we were all excited at the idea of finally meeting little Emma Danielle. We had been waiting so long to see her and hold her, cuddle her, kiss her cheeks and tell her how much we loved her. It had been a long pregnancy with lots of morning sickness, backaches and pulled muscles. I was definitely ready for this little one to come out and meet us.

Friday, March 11<u>th</u> - Labor & Delivery

When we arrived at the birthing center, Charlotte (our wonderful midwife for delivery), met us at the door. We got the kids settled and Johnny and I headed to one of the birthing rooms to prepare for labor. We figured it would be a tough night but knew it would have a wonderful ending with Emma's arrival.

When Charlotte started examining me, I was dilated to about four centimeters and effaced about halfway. She felt my belly to determine Emma's position and started searching for Emma's heartbeat with the fetal doppler. We did not hear anything. She moved the doppler to a different position, but she still could not find her heartbeat. We tried multiple positions for several minutes and even tried to find a visual on the heartbeat with an ultrasound but to no avail.

As Charlotte walked out of the room to make a call, Johnny thought that Emma was just in a weird position but I had a sinking feeling in my stomach. "Start calling people and praying," I told him. He kept assuring me that all would be well. Emma was just not cooperating with her positioning.

When Charlotte came back into the room, she suggested that we head to the nearest hospital, thinking that she could not find a heartbeat because of her technique. But, I could tell that something was wrong. Charlotte was panicking. She was hiding it well, but I could see the panic in her actions and hear it in her voice. I again told Johnny to start calling people and he needed to start praying. I was already in prayer, constant prayer, mentally on my knees asking the Lord to help our baby.

We gathered up the kids, loaded up the Tahoe once more and headed to the hospital. In less than ten minutes I was hooked up to a fetal heart monitor ... but still no heartbeat. The doctor came in and tried the ultrasound, but he could not find the heartbeat either.

"Are you sure?" I asked him.

He called in the radiologist who confirmed it, "I am sorry, ma'am, but your baby has no heartbeat."

"Oh, God! Nooooo!!!!" I cried as sobs of aching pain took over. Johnny had been standing next to me. As the doctor delivered the news, Johnny looked at me and the first words he said were, "It's not your fault." I felt him wrap his arm around me and I leaned into him. His head came down on top of mine and we just clung to each other and cried. I could not think of anything at all except that I would never hear Emma cry or giggle or even see her smile. All my dreams of Emma dissolved in the salty tears that ran down my cheeks. I would never know if she had blue eyes or brown or feel her grab my finger in her tiny fist, nor would I get to change her diaper, not even once. She would not fall asleep on my chest and our midnight feedings would never take place. The long nights filled with baby cries would now be silent nights.

Losing Emma

As Johnny stepped out of the room to make calls, I heard him say to the first person who answered, "We need you. We lost Emma." Then he was out the door asking people to start praying and gathering for us.

We knew that we needed people. Now was the time for all the prayers we could get. We needed prayer warriors to storm the gates of heaven for us, hoping for a miracle that Emma could be brought back, to protect us in our time of need, to just be with us and surround us with love.

As he stepped out, Charlotte stepped in and held me. By this time another midwife had joined us, Samantha, and she cried with us.

Tears flooded the room as my shattered heart lay in a thousand pieces on the floor. I remember asking Charlotte and Samantha, "How do we plan a funeral for a baby that hasn't been born yet?"

"Don't think about that now," they answered, but that is all that went through my mind. The nurse brought me a tiny box of Kleenex. That little bitty box was not going to cut it. The baby-sized tissues would have been great for weepy eyes, but not for my flood of tears.

I do not know how many times I heard, "I am so sorry." I know it is difficult for people to understand how it feels and I know they are at a loss of words. There are truly no words that others can offer to help the pain and there are no words mothers can use to describe their pain. Although the thoughts and feelings are well placed, sorry just does not seem to cut it when your unborn infant lies dead in your womb.

Heartbreaking and sorrowful do not even begin to describe the initial pain in my heart, the emptiness I felt inside. After eight long months of preparation, prayer and joy we were down to the final hours before Emma was to be born knowing that she would never take her first breath. I felt as if a part of me died the moment we found out she was going to be stillborn, as if a light inside had been extinguished and snuffed out. The overwhelming feeling of loss, devastation and sorrow seemed to engulf and surround my heart, suffocating my very soul. The bottles, diapers, baby clothes and shampoos that I had gathered for Emma would not be used. The hopes and dreams I had for her, the love that I had been planning on lavishing her with, lay on the floor of the hospital room, shattered and broken like shards of glass.

What I did not know at that point, was that God's plans were already well in motion. Emma's purpose for dying and our testimony to God's love for us had just begun and were about to take on a life of their own.

Yes, we were devastated.
Yes, we were heartbroken.
Yes, God was in control.

Labor Continues

Through the sorrow and pain, labor continued. I was moved to a labor and delivery room in a secluded corner of the maternity floor. In fact, we were in the very last room at the end of a long hallway. I am not sure if that was more for our privacy or for the other women in labor on the floor. We found out later that fourteen other women had come throughout the morning to deliver their babies. The maternity floor was bursting at the seams with joyous families who were bringing healthy babies into the world. We were the only ones in the hospital that had experienced a stillbirth that day and we were the first stillbirth for the birthing center in about a year.

With gentle kindness and weepy eyes, the nurses came in, took my vitals and prepared me for delivery. We decided that the best option at this point was to make me as comfortable as possible, to not feel the pain of childbirth.

This was supposed to be my first natural childbirth experience. With James and Lauren, I had epidurals and typical hospital births. However, I wanted something different for this delivery. I wanted to try it naturally, which is why I chose the birthing center with the staff of midwives. They were excellent during my entire pregnancy and I have never regretted going that route, even to this day. God bless my sweet daddy and mother-in-law. Both of them were very concerned that we chose the birthing center instead of a hospital. Even though we ended up at a hospital, I was still at peace with our decision with the birthing center.

The nurse said that we could start the epidural and petocin as soon as I was ready. I told her it was time. There was no use prolonging what I knew was already coming. Emma was already in heaven, her body simply needed to be born. Within a short time the epidural was working and later the petocin was started (to further jump start delivery).

While we waited for labor to progress, my sister, Charlsye, her husband, Chris, and my Dad and stepmother, Linda, sat in the room with us. I remember feeling very calm at certain times and then tears just streaming down my face as the next wave of grief crashed in on me. Through it all, though, I still had to deliver Emma. That thought alone was very sobering. I kept thinking that I had to make sure I focused on her delivery, to make it as special as possible. I wanted to remember everything as my memories of her would be held to that moment since we would not have any other time with her while here on earth.

It was the quietest birth I have ever had. With both James and Lauren certain songs played over and over in my head throughout delivery. I am not sure why these particular songs popped in my head. With James it was "Devil Down in Georgia" and with Lauren it was classical music. When I was practicing the Bradley breathing techniques several weeks before delivery, I tried to visualize myself in a different setting (like a beach or eating something delicious like melted chocolate). Those things did not work. The sandy beach made me feel dirty and nasty and the thought of chocolate made me hungry. But the children's song, *Jesus Loves Me*, popped into my head. That is the song that played in my head while we were in transit from the house to the birthing center and then again it played in my mind a few times during delivery at the hospital.

My family sat in the room with us, talking, holding hands, and giving hugs. At one point I looked at Charlsye and told her I felt a lot of pressure. Everyone was cleared out of the room and three pushes later, Emma was born at 8:18 a.m. weighing six pounds, six ounces and measuring nineteen and one-half inches long. As she was delivered, we discovered the cause of her death. The umbilical cord had been wrapped around her neck three times.

There was no rushing around with a screaming newborn, cleaning her eyes, clearing her lungs or bathing her to have her bundled up and placed on my chest. Instead, it was calm and peaceful. Emma was quietly born into this world and our family. While the doctor took care of me, the nurse placed Emma on my chest and Johnny, for the first time, cut the cord. The tears in his eyes said it all: pain and sorrow mixed with all the love in his heart.

About this time, I had excessive bleeding and started hemorrhaging. The nurse took Emma to clean her. Johnny's face grew intense with fear. He later told me that he could not lose both of us, that he needed me and so did James and Lauren. He kept going back and forth between me and Emma, making sure I was okay and watching as the nurse cleaned up Emma.

He has always been a protective father and was just as protective over Emma, even though we knew she was already in heaven. Daddy's have instincts, too, instincts to protect and love. My hemorrhaging stopped. Physically I was going to be okay. Emotionally, I was still raw.

Emma was beautiful. My heart ached at seeing her for the first time but my love for her poured out in the tears that ran down my cheeks. She had Johnny's puffy cheeks, a cleft chin like her brother and me, Lauren's lips and "swirly" hair (as Charlsye called it). She had more hair than either James or Lauren had when they were born. I just know she was going to have curly hair like me. I never saw the color of her eyes, but I know they would have been blue like mine. Johnny thinks they were going to be brown like his. James and Lauren also have brown eyes like Johnny, but Emma, sweet Emma was going to have blue eyes just like her mama. And her feet ... my goodness her feet were so small and so soft. I could have rubbed them forever. With James, it was his hands and with Lauren I loved to rub her hair, but with Emma it was her feet. She also had long fingers like her big brother, James. I did not see it right away, but over the next twenty-four hours, I came to see a lot of Johnny's grandmother in her face. She was definitely a good mixture of all of us, her family. She was simply beautiful.

Once Emma and I were both cleaned and ready for visitors, our families came in. Dad, Linda, Charlsye and Chris were already there but a little bit later Johnny's parents, Joe and Betty, his brother, Danny and his sister, Teresa, arrived. Emma was passed around so that everyone could hold her and tell us how beautiful she was. She was cradled, kissed and rocked, just as all newborns should be. We had her wrapped in the blanket that James and Lauren had chosen for her, dark brown with colorful big polka dots on it. It was so soft, just perfect for a newborn.

It is not just the parents that mourn the loss of a child, but entire families. Brothers or sisters may not understand why their baby sister did not come home from the hospital. Grandparents grieve for the grandchild they will never get to spoil. Aunts and uncles lament for the niece or nephew they will never get to hold or cuddle or babysit. No one is immune from the loss of a child.

It seemed as if Johnny was on the phone with people almost all day. We never realized how many friends and family we had, but we definitely appreciated all the love and support we received.

The amazing thing is that in January, two short months before Emma's birth, Johnny started to reconnect with the people in our lives: rebuild friendships, repair relationships, and just become more involved. We had become so engrossed with our everyday living that we had disconnected from others. Life was too busy between homeschooling, working, gardening, canning, etc. Those were excuses, though. God intended for people to be together, to help each other, to love one another. There are many instances in the Bible where Jesus called the disciples His friends. In fact, Jesus said in John 15:13, "Greater love has no one than this, than to lay down one's life for his friends."

Johnny made a commitment to be a better friend and he started reaching out to our friends and telling them, "I need you. I am reconnecting with you. Let's get together sometime." Had he not done this, it would have been a lonely time for us at the hospital.

Little did we know in January that two months later we would rely on those friendships and family relationships to see us through the most difficult situation in our lives.

The Holy Spirit at the Hospital

All day visitors came and went, our wonderful friends from church and later some of our thoughtful co-workers from the office. As they came in, they were greeted at the door by the Holy Spirit, who ushered them in and spoke to their hearts, cloaking them in the same peace and love that embraced us.

We would see the tears in their eyes, feel their sorrow in their hugs and kisses and know that they needed to hear what we had to proclaim: Emma was in heaven and Jesus was rocking our baby for us. I am not saying that we did not still feel the grief of losing our precious baby. I am saying that God was in control and He had our baby with Him in heaven. The glory that we seek to have one day was hers *now*! God had given us peace "which surpasses all understanding," (Philippians 4:7) so that as Christ comforted us in our grief, we could then in turn comfort others.

We said from the beginning that Emma was our miracle baby. But the miracles came through her death, not her birth. It was because of her death that we have a wonderful testimony of Christ's love for us and for others.

The Holy Spirit was in the room with us and had been with us from the moment we found out Emma was to be stillborn. As I mentioned earlier, I felt a sense of overwhelming loss but even in my despair, I still had peace. The light that I believed had been snuffed out glowed brighter and brighter as the day wore on. John 14:26 says the Holy Spirit is the "Helper" (can also be translated as Comforter) and Luke 12:12 says, "For the Holy Spirit will teach you in that very hour what you ought to say." The Holy Spirit helped to guide our tongues and words that day, lifting up not only us, but even those who entered our room, from the hospital staff to our friends and co-workers. In Acts 1:8 Jesus says that when the Holy Spirit comes upon you, you shall be witnesses to Him to the end of the earth. Those words are so true even today. The Holy Spirit poured through us into the lives of others and in doing so we were able to be witnesses to Jesus' love.

When my mother-in-law, Betty, came into the room that morning, she gave me a hug and I asked, "How are you doing? Are you okay?" She looked at me through the tears in her eyes and said,

"I should be asking you that." We do not blame God for what happened. Instead, we thank Him for taking her home where she will never suffer, nor will she know evil or pain.

Because of the Holy Spirit and God's grace, Johnny was able to lovingly show each visitor our sweet Emma. He would introduce her, "This is Emma." With tender hands he unwrapped her blankets and proudly showed her soft little feet, long fingers and swirly hair, telling the visitor all about Emma. I fell deeper in love with him each and every time. With gentle hands, he bundled her back up and asked if she wanted to hold Emma. He was so proud of her and he wanted everyone to know that this was his daughter. Johnny's always been a good father, but I was never more proud of my husband than during that day. All of my children have such a wonderful father.

March 12, 2011 – Going Home

I was discharged from the hospital late Saturday afternoon. Aside from delivering Emma, the hardest thing was leaving her at the hospital. We prepared Emma for when the funeral home came to pick her up. She wore the little outfit that James and Lauren chose as her "going home" outfit, only now her body was going to the funeral home, not our home. We wrapped her in the blanket that my mother had crocheted for her. It fit her perfectly as mom did not finish it before Emma was born. My co-workers had brought us yellow roses on Friday so we took one of those roses and placed it in her folded hands. We then laid over her the little white crocheted blanket that the hospital gave us. We also left a pink bow for her head and a white pair of socks for the funeral home to put on her later. She looked so peaceful.

I wanted to take her home with me, not leave her there. After all, parents are not supposed to leave their newborn at the hospital. She was supposed to be strapped in her car seat and bundled up for her journey home. Babies are supposed to sleep in their freshly prepared beds, to be fed and snuggled, kissed and hugged. They are not to be buried so young, but life does not always work out the way we hope or think it will.

Nevertheless, Johnny and I walked out of the hospital, hand in hand. Ecclesiastes 4:9-12 says:

> *Two are better than one, because they have a good reward for their labor. For if they fall, one will lift up his companion. But woe to him who is alone when he falls, for he has no one to help him up.*

> Again, if two lie down together, they will keep warm; but how can one be warm alone? Though one may be overpowered by another, two can withstand him. And a threefold cord is not quickly broken.

We walked with God leading us, creating our strongly held threefold cord. We knew that God had a plan for us.

When we reached the car, Emma's birthday cake was sitting in my seat – untouched. In all the commotion, I had forgotten about it. It was a sad reminder of the birthdays that would never occur for Emma. We took the birthday cake back home, sliced it up and put it in the freezer. It became our snack of choice over the next few weeks. It was as if we were celebrating her heavenly birth every time we ate a piece. From now on, March 11th will be a day of remembrance for little Emma with Lemon Bundt Cake as a tasty memorial to our sweet angel.

The Funeral

Planning a funeral is difficult. It is emotionally draining trying to determine the burial clothes, picking out the funeral home, the music, writing the eulogy and the list goes on. Multiply those emotions and feelings by a thousand percent and that is how we felt planning Emma's funeral.

In the days after leaving the hospital Johnny and I were on auto pilot, at least it seemed we were. We ate, slept, took care of James and Lauren and lived from one moment to the next, not really looking past the minute we were in. We would take some time to be alone with our thoughts and emotions, grieving our sweet little baby. Those were tender days for us. We held each other close and cried with each other, truly loving and nurturing each other in our grief. We read God's Word to each other and focused on the details of life itself.

We tried to keep the days as normal as possible for James and Lauren, but even they understood that this was a life-altering event for our family.

A few days before Emma's memorial service, we wanted to go to the funeral home to see her one more time, to make sure that she was laid out the way we wanted. I thought this would be one of the more difficult days, but God's peace was on us. I can't stress that enough. *God's peace was on us.* It turned out to be a touching time for Johnny and me.

She looked like a beautiful, tiny angel. I know she was small but I did not realize just how diminutive she was until I saw the basket on the table in the viewing room. Emma was bundled up in her "made just for her" pink blanket with the pink bow encircling her head like a halo. Johnny carefully removed Emma's blankets until he could see her feet, which were adorned with the white socks we left for her. They were the same socks that both James and Lauren had worn when they were infants, but they seemed to engulf Emma's soft petite feet. Her beautiful swirly hair had been combed down so we tousled it a bit. After all, she would have been a country girl and country girls have tousled hair. We told her we loved her and spent some time just memorizing her features, gently rubbing her feet and stroking her hair. We were giving her love the only way we could, just as any parents would do to their newborn. I will never forget how peaceful she looked and how God's peace and love surrounded us.

Emma's funeral was one week to the day of her death, March 18th. I remember waking up that morning and praying, "Lord, please give me the strength I need to get through today." As it turned out, it was a beautiful, sunny spring day in Texas and as always, God gave me what I needed to get through the day (and then some). I should have expected no less.

We live in the middle of acreage and our driveway is not what you would call a normal road. It is extremely gutted and weathered with ruts the size of the Grand Canyon. We were being chauffeured that day and there was no way that our driver would be able to get the limousine down that washed out, weather-beaten road. We left the house a little early and leisurely walked up to the highway to meet him. Along the way Lauren picked wildflowers and by the time we reached the highway, she had a little bouquet (which she later placed on Emma's casket).

This world is indeed small. It turned out that our driver's sister is the longest standing member of our beekeeping association. This retired pastor is now a chauffeur for the funeral home. He was one of God's angels sent to be with us that day. He kept us entertained with stories of Georgetown from "back in the day." God blessed us with just the right chauffeur for our special day. Again, I should have expected no less.

As for the funeral itself, it was simply beautiful. We knew what we wanted for Emma, but the most important message we wanted people to understand is that God loves them. We discovered during our short time in grief that we can either let our light shine for Christ or be tormented by the darkness. We chose to live in the light. In fact, part of the eulogy that Johnny and I wrote was based on what we felt Emma had to say in her passing:

> *"And most of all she wanted to remind people that they should turn on their lights. She's probably giggling as she sees the looks on your faces right about now, but she said, 'Make sure they turn the light up all the way. Let your light shine everywhere you go. Be a light to the world so that others may know Christ.'"*

Her funeral was one of celebration, not sorrow. It was a joyous memorial service honoring Emma's passage to heaven, knowing that she would be waiting for us. When *I'll Fly Away* was sung, it was with an upbeat tempo, not as a funeral dirge. You could feel the joy in the church. I shed not one tear during the entire service. I could not because I did not feel sorrow, but pure joy. It sounds strange, but the Holy Spirit was still continuing to move through us.

Brother Dan spoke such beautiful words and stories from the Bible. We wanted others to know Jesus like we do and Dan did a remarkable job of conveying God's love to those in attendance (his message starts on page 47).

One story Dan mentioned in his message is that sometimes shepherds have problems getting their flocks to cross streams or rivers when the sheep think the passage will be difficult or dangerous. However, if the shepherd can coax a lamb or ewe to cross first, then the rest of the sheep follow. Dan equated it to children passing on into heaven first. Although we know heaven is a wonderful place, it makes it even more inviting to know that we have a child waiting for us.

As we were leaving the church for the cemetery, David Denson, a Sheriff's Deputy and one of our good friends, asked if he could lead the escort to the grave site. It was such an honor to us that he asked. With David's squad car in the lead and four or five other motorcycle cops helping with traffic control, we made our way to Emma's final resting place. At Johnny's request, we drove by our gate so that we could show Emma where she would have lived. It was the closest she ever came to going home with us.

I am not sure about other states but here in Texas, when a funeral procession goes by, other drivers on the road pull over until the procession has passed, out of respect for the deceased and the family. I have been in funeral processions before, but never like this. It was an amazing sight as first one car and then another pulled to the side of the highway as we passed. It was definitely different to experience the respect from the perspective of the grieving family rather than as a passerby.

There was one bystander I will never forget. This gentleman not only pulled over, but got out and stood "at ease" next to his car. You could tell from his appearance that he was a former soldier. He had no idea this was the funeral for a newborn, but regardless of who might have been in the hearse, he nonetheless stood at ease. My heart swelled with pride for sweet Emma but I was also very humbled by the awesome respect he not only gave to Emma, but us as well. Many people mentioned him to us for days and weeks following Emma's funeral.

I thought her funeral would be one of the hardest days, but in fact, it was one of the most beautiful. Johnny and I felt like we honored both God and Emma that day. We poured a lifetime of love into her service and burial arrangements. To do any less would have been a dishonor.

God's Word on Death

We all know that death is a normal part of life. Even though no one really wants to talk about it or deal with it, we all face the reality of death at some point, whether it is parents, grandparents, children, aunts, uncles or friends that pass away. I have mourned the loss of aunts, uncles and grandparents, but losing Emma brought me to a whole new level of grief and sorrow. To this day I feel as if a part of our family is missing. I looked forward to those sleepless nights and all the "firsts" that we would not experience (first time to roll over, crawl, walk, laugh, and all the rest). As a mama, I truly miss Emma and cry out to God to heal my hurting heart (and He does, a little bit every single day).

But, despite my pain and sorrow, I take comfort from God's Word, which says that the dead only sleep until Jesus returns when all will be alive again and those who believe will be resurrected to eternal life.

First Corinthians 15:20-22 says, "But now Christ is risen from the dead, and has become the firstfruits of those who have fallen asleep. For since by man came death, by man also came the resurrection of the dead. For as in Adam all die, even so in Christ all shall be made alive." Christ died on the cross, conquered death and ascended into heaven. He was the first and only one to have done this, but He paved the way for the rest of the believers to follow. Adam and Eve sinned and because of their sin, the rest of the world died to sin (as the wages of sin is death) (Romans 6:13). However, through Christ's death and resurrection, those who believe in Jesus and have put their trust and faith in Him shall have eternal life.

In the meantime, the dead simply sleep. King David wrote about the "sleep of death" in Psalm 13:3, "Consider and hear me, O Lord my God; enlighten my eyes, lest I sleep the sleep of death." Or consider what Daniel said, "And many of those who sleep in the dust of the earth shall awake" (Daniel 12:2). Isaiah 26:19 says, "Your dead shall live; together with my dead body they shall arise. Awake and sing, you who dwell in dust." Even Genesis 3:19 says the bodies of the dead shall return to the dust from which they came, but as believers in Christ, we know that we will live eternally (1 John 5:11).

Family Pictures

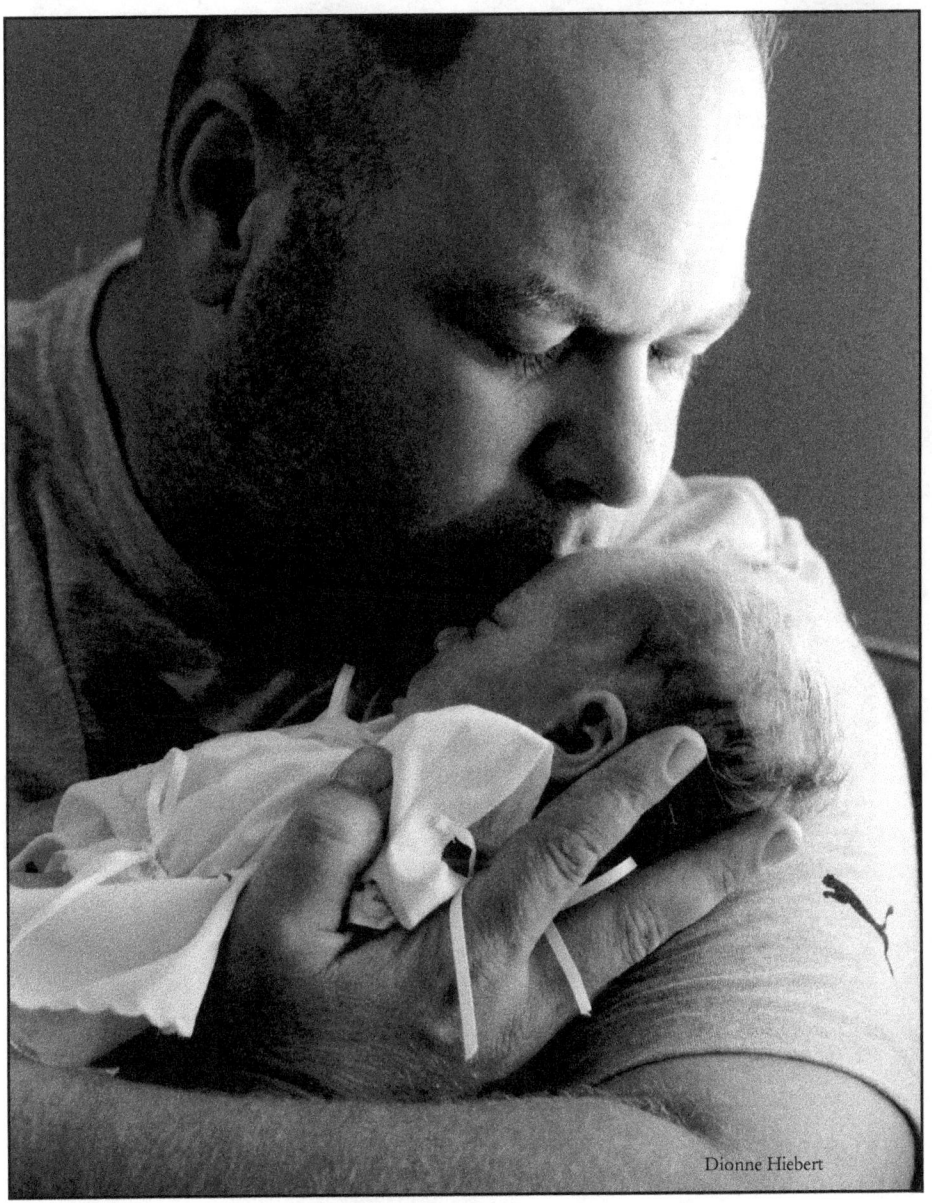

Johnny and Emma

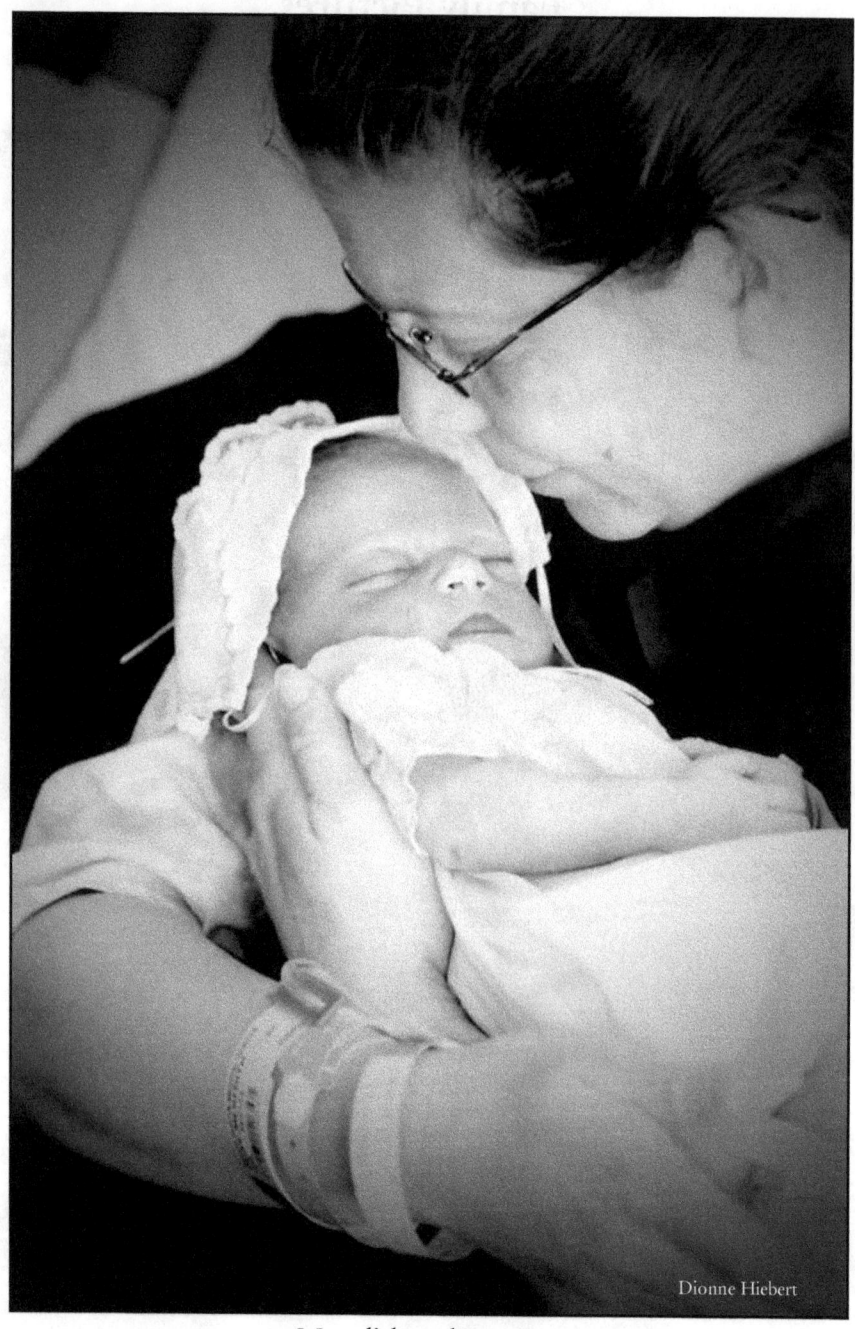

Meredith and Emma

Family Pictures

March 9th –
The day before
labor started

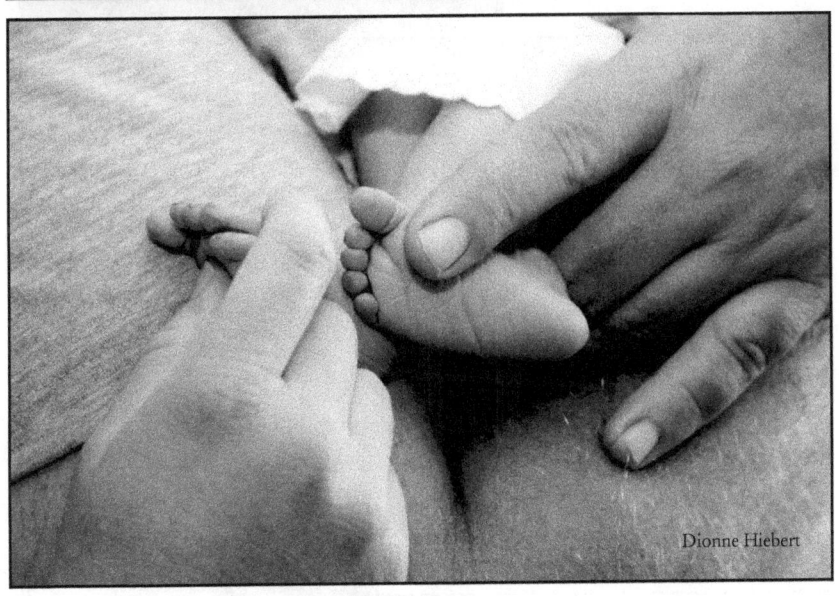

Emma's Precious Feet

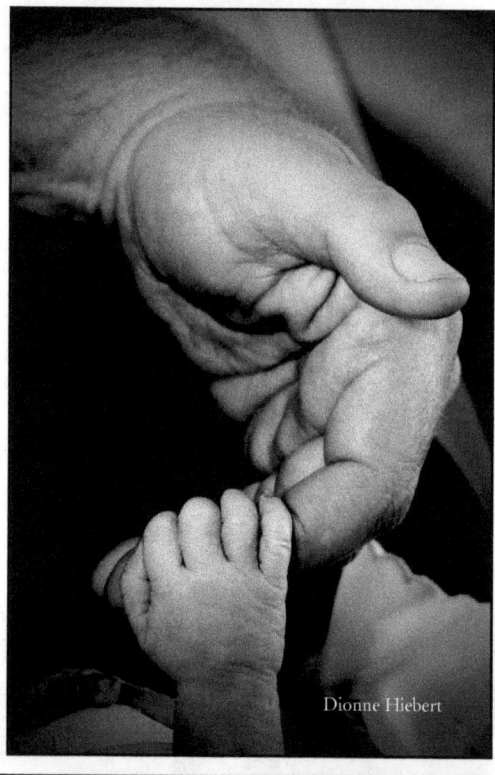

Emma's Memorial Box

Emma's Tiny Casket

The Duke Family 2011

Chapter 3
Walking on the Water with Jesus

Now faith is the substance of things hoped for, the evidence of things not seen. – Hebrews 11:1

Without faith, accepting Emma's death would have been impossible, but as Philippians 4:13 says, "I can do all things through Christ who strengthens me." Through faith and by God's love and grace, we will see Emma again when we are united in heaven. Do you realize that the words "by faith" are written 18 times in Hebrews 11? By faith we understand that God created the world out of things not seen. By faith Abel offered God a better sacrifice and received his blessing. By faith Noah built an ark and saved his family from the flood. By faith Abraham left his home country and traveled to a foreign land, not knowing where he was going, but following God's plan for him. By faith Sarah "received strength to conceive seed; and she bore a child when she was past the age, because she judged Him faithful who had promised" (Hebrews 11:11). By faith Isaac blessed Jacob and Esau. By faith, Jacob blessed his twelve sons. By faith Rahab (the harlot) "did not perish with those who did not believe, when she had received the spies with peace" (Hebrews 11:31). And the list goes on and on. *By faith* these believers did as God directed them and received their blessings from Him.

By faith, Johnny and I know that there is a purpose for Emma's passing. By faith we walk with God every single day. By faith we continue trust in God and His plans for us.

Do you remember earlier when I said that God was in control? While it may not have been clear right away, God's plan for Emma was slowly revealed to us shortly after her birth.

My Faith Growing Up

Before I go any further, let me explain that I had been on a faith journey for several months. I have always believed in God and have known Jesus since I was a little girl. We went to church and Sunday School every week when I was growing up and I heard and believed all the stories about Jesus. He has always been a part of my family as He is my heavenly Father.

Psalm 27:1 says, "The Lord is my light and my salvation; whom shall I fear? The Lord is the strength of my life; of whom shall I be afraid?" These words resonate with me for many reasons and I turn to these words quite often, but I especially did so during my "growing up" years.

When I was fourteen, God was with me when my Mom left us. I leaned on Him during those impressionable high school years. He blessed me with many other motherly role models that I could turn to during that time. He knew what I needed long before I ever did and put Godly women in my life that would help me along the way.

About three years later, I was home alone and attempting to go to sleep. For some reason, I had this enormous fear within me, holding me captive. I must have passionately and fervently prayed for at least thirty minutes (probably more) for God to give me peace and protect me. At one point during my prayers, I felt as if I was being picked up and cradled. A peace like I had never experienced before washed over me. My fears immediately ceased and I fell asleep like a baby. God cradled me in His loving arms, just as if I were a small child again in my daddy's arms, only this time I was a teenager in my heavenly Father's arms.

Then again in 1993, as a junior in college, I was taking a flight to Canada for a week-long Literature course. Typically I do not fear flying. However, fear was holding me hostage again that day. I prayed for our safety while we were waiting to enter the plane, while we were finding our seats, and all during take-off. When we emerged above the clouds, I looked out the window (still praying) and I could see the shadow of the plane on the clouds below us. It was encircled in a complete and perfect rainbow. Some might say that it was due to a scientific reason, but no, it was God. He gave me a sign that He was with me, protecting me once again. He calmed my fears with that simple rainbow and I was at peace for the rest of the trip.

Those were not the only times He was with me. I can count many others, but these stand out in my mind the most.

I strongly believe that after all I have been through in my life, I am who I am today because of my experiences and my growing relationship with Jesus Christ. It is the difficult struggles in life that bring us closer to God and Jesus. That is when we truly understand God's love for us.

My Faith Journey with Emma

About eight weeks before Emma was born I was heading into the office one morning and caught part of a sermon by Charles Stanley on the radio[2]. He was explaining the story of Peter walking on the water towards Jesus (Matthew 14: 24-32). When Peter got out of the boat, with his eyes on Jesus, he walked on the water towards the Lord. But, when he took his eyes off Jesus, Peter noticed the waves and stormy seas and started to sink. His faith faltered because he did not keep His eyes on the Lord. He was going to drown in his faithlessness, but Jesus reached out to Peter and caught him by the hand. The point is we can all drown in our faithlessness. We must keep our eyes on Jesus and grab onto His hand when He offers it.

I thought about that sermon all day. We need to get out of the boat like Peter and walk on the water with Jesus. If our eyes are on Him, everything else disappears – the waves, the stormy seas, all the distractions that cause us to sink.

When I got home that night, I found the sermon on Mr. Stanley's website and played it for Johnny. I needed him to understand that I was ready to walk on the water with Jesus. I needed to practice my faith and put it in Jesus' hands. I wanted to quit my job of thirteen years following Emma's birth and actually be a full-time mama.

When James was born in 1998, Johnny stayed at home while I returned to work. We decided that when Lauren was born we would switch and he would return to work and I would stay at home with James and Lauren. The morning I found out I was pregnant with Lauren, I gave nine months notice. I eventually arranged with the office to work from home as an independent contractor following Lauren's birth. Up until Emma was born I was working about thirty hours a week plus homeschooling, gardening, canning, etc. It was an enormous load to carry but I did it with God's grace and strength (as I would not have been able to do it all on my own).

When I told Johnny that I wanted to quit entirely, he told me that I could do whatever I needed to do. He would support me in my decision, whatever it was.

It was a hard decision for me. January 2011 marked my thirteenth anniversary with this company and nine of those years I worked from home handling marketing, programming and presentations. For years I thought of this job as our security blank that had held us

---

[2] Charles Stanley. In-Touch Ministries. Archive title: When We Say Yes – Part 1. Dated January 13, 2011. http://www.intouch.org/broadcast/audio-archives

together financially while my husband was in real estate or landscaping. It fed us and paid our bills while Johnny's businesses ramped up. Quitting was one of the hardest decisions I had ever made and it was a decision I did not make lightly.

But in reality, the Lord provided for us, not this job. Yes, He provided the job for me, but in truth, it was and is all God, not me and not the company that paid our bills and kept us fed.

A week after our conversation I was again driving into the office and kept thinking about that same "get out of the boat" sermon. I felt truly convicted that God wanted me to quit and stay at home full time. When I got to the office, I immediately called Johnny and told him that I was giving my notice that day. I could not wait another day. What I did not know is that he had been trying to reach me on my way in to the office. We had not really talked about it since our conversation the week before but his first response to me was, "Good. I have been trying to reach you on your way in to tell you to give your notice." God was speaking to Johnny's heart that morning, too. We were on the same page and that felt so good and so incredibly right.

Without delay, I met with my boss and gave my resignation to be effective the day of Emma's birth. I was asked not to leave, but I felt that I had really made the right decision, that God had led me to this decision. I was convicted in my heart that I was doing the right thing and felt that my decision was blessed. I knew that because my eyes were on Jesus. I was walking on the water with my Lord and Savior. Little did I know that seven weeks later little Emma would be in heaven and the waves would start crashing in on me.

It was around this time that we were visiting some of our dear friends, David and Christina Denson. It was a wonderful visit and very heartwarming. We spent a long time talking about faith and where God was leading us as families. At some point we talked about books we had been reading. David went and grabbed his copy of the book *Heaven is for Real*[3] by Todd Burpo. If you are not familiar with this book, it explains 4-year old Colton Burpo's journey to heaven when his spirit left his body on the operating room table during emergency surgery. It is an amazing book. As Christians we believe the Bible as it is written in its entirety but it really helped us to understand and see heaven from a child's perspective – to be able to

---

3 Burpo, Todd. *Heaven is for Real: A Little Boy's Astounding Story of His Trip to Heaven and Back.* Colorado: Thomas Nelson, 2010.

visualize the beautiful place where Emma now lives eternally. Colton explained the beautiful colors, colors that do not exist down here on earth, on the gems, rainbows and sashes that the people wore. He also said that there were lots of children and that Jesus had the prettiest eyes.

From the moment we found out that Emma was going to be stillborn, we knew in our hearts that she was already with Jesus and He was rocking her for us. In fact, that is what I told everyone who visited us. The description of heaven from Colton's point of view really hit home with us. *THIS* is where Emma eternally lives! No pain, no sorrow, no heartache or grief. She is in the best place of all! She is where we strive to be one day! My baby is in heaven!

With our eyes on Jesus, we were walking on the water with Him, first with quitting my job and then with Emma. Do you see a pattern here? As long as our eyes are on Jesus, the things of this world disappear.

God Knows Your Pain

You may have lost your child through miscarriage, stillbirth, ectopic pregnancy, abortion, SIDS, illness or disease or even through a terrible accident. Your baby may have never breathed his first breath or she may have been 19 years old. Outliving your child is devastating no matter how old you are or how old your child is.

But there is one who knows how it feels and His child was thirty-three years old. He watched as His Son was scourged, mocked, nailed to a cross and crucified. Through all the torture and brutality, God the Father silently watched. As a parent, it must have pained Him to see His beloved Son suffer for you and me. I am surprised He did not cry a river of tears.

Do you realize that God has the same love for you? He wants you to come to Him, to love Him. He loves us so much that He sent his only Son so that by believing in Him (Jesus) we will never perish but have eternal life (John 3:16).

Emma is now living her eternal life with Jesus. As it says in Ecclesiastes 4:3, "Yet, better than both is he who has never existed, who has not seen the evil work that is done under the sun." Emma existed in my womb. She was a part of me physically for nine months. She will always be my baby and my daughter. But, I'll never have to see her suffer or grieve and she'll never know the evil of this world. She is truly in the best place she could ever be, in Jesus' loving arms.

I take my sorrow to God every day knowing that He understands my pain and grief. He understands because He lived through it with Jesus. He hears my cry and comforts my heart. He cradles me in His loving arms and fills my aching soul with His love. My heart breaks open and His tender hands put it back together. He's my healer and comforter.

Revelation 21:4 says, "And God will wipe away every tear from their eyes; there shall be no more death, nor sorrow, nor crying. There shall be no more pain, for the former things have passed away." That's a beautiful promise of what awaits us in heaven. Through God's love for us and Jesus' victory over death, that victory is also ours (1 Corinthians 16:19). While we may cry and mourn here on earth, one day our tears will be wiped away and the former things will pass away.

In the Cemetery

I think of Jesus and God's love for us when I walk through the cemetery. Before Emma's death, I never really paid much attention to the headstones, let alone spent much time in a cemetery. However, now I really notice all of the infants and young children who died many years ago. Once upon a time their mothers and fathers grieved for them just as we grieve for Emma now. Mothers probably sat on the hard ground next to a newly buried child and cried out to God, just as I have done.

Fathers may have planted flowers or a tree in memory of their beloved children, just as Johnny has done. Headstones tell a sad tale for some families – infants and toddlers lay side by side in their graves with their parents' graves next to them. One family lost two young children very close together. The devastation those families felt must have been pure anguish. I can only hope that the mother and father had accepted Christ and are now happily united with their children in heaven.

Or consider another family whose three children all died within a few years of each other. One was an infant, another a small child and the third was ten years old. The father committed suicide five years after the third child died. The only reason we know this is through meeting a descendant of the family at a chance encounter while visiting Emma's grave. The grief of the wife and mother must have been hard. Were they saved? Did they know Jesus? Did they have a relationship with Him?

Chapter 4
Emma's Journal, Eulogy & Message

For each of our children, I have kept a journal for them since the day I found out I was pregnant. It is my way of telling them how much I love them from the beginning until they are an adult. I even have one for my first pregnancy that ended in a miscarriage after seven weeks.

I wanted to share my thoughts and prayers for Emma with you, in the hopes that you can truly understand how Emma blessed our lives right from the very beginning.

For our precious little baby – my thoughts during my pregnancy with you! I want you to know how much I love you and think about you – even while you're in my womb ... always in my thoughts, prayers and heart.
Love,
Mom

September 6, 2010
Hello, Baby Duke! You haven't been born yet but one day soon you will be. You have an older brother (James) and an older sister (Lauren). By the time you're born, James will be twelve and Lauren will be nine. As for you, my sweet baby, you won't be born for another six months.

This journal is for you ... my thoughts on this pregnancy, how I am feeling, what the doctor has to say – EVERYTHING! It'll especially include my thoughts about you! We are all very excited – that's for sure!

I will honestly tell you that you were a surprise. I thought we weren't going to have any more children but God had other plans. You came along! Dad was in shock for about two weeks – honestly.

September 8, 2010
Not much sleep last night, little one. We had seven to ten inches of rain yesterday and very early into this morning. The rain was so loud last night that it kept me up. The wind was incredibly strong as

well. The good news is that we needed the rain and the break from the heat.

Aside from the weather, all is well. My morning sickness (which has plagued me from almost the beginning of this pregnancy) has pretty much gone away. Praise the Lord! That has got to be one of the worst feelings in the world. I know that you are well worth the morning sickness but it's just not very fun.

Right now we do not know if you're a girl or a boy. Dad and I think you are a girl. James is hoping for a little brother and Lauren would love a baby sister. I do know one thing – whether you are a boy or a girl you will be loved very much. You already are.

September 12, 2010

I am now 14 weeks. Yeah! The morning sickness hit with a vengeance today. I really wish that it would go away and that I would feel better. Throwing up is not fun!

September 16, 2010

Hello, baby! We were kicking around baby names last night. If you happen to be a boy, we like Adam and Jacob.

September 19, 2010

I am at 15 weeks now. Five more weeks and we'll find out if God blessed us with a girl or a boy. That's so exciting! I've been suffering with a major headache for the past two days. That's no fun at all. It's kind of going away now but I still feel a twinge of pain. Hopefully it'll go away sometime today. I've been looking at a lot of baby things – highchairs, strollers, car seats, baby tubs, etc. We've been hunting everywhere for the nuts and bolts to your baby bed but haven't found them yet. I am hoping they'll turn up somewhere soon. Otherwise we'll have to improvise. Hmmm....

September 26, 2010

As I read the Bible this morning I cannot help but think of you – my unborn babe. There are so many things that you will learn once you are here with me and your family. The most important things I want you to know go beyond walking and manners and sitting up. You are a child of God – first and foremost. David says in Psalm 139:13-16:

For you created my inmost being; you knit me together in my mother's womb. I praise you because I am fearfully and wonderfully made; your works are wonderful. I know that full well. My frame was not hidden from you when I was made in the secret place. When I was woven together in the depths of the earth, your eyes saw my unformed body. All the days ordained for me were written in your book before one of them came to be.

As long as you live, oh precious babe of mine – always know that God loves you, designed you and knew you before I ever did. You are His. He has simply blessed my life with you – to raise you as one of His own. It's a great honor for me and I cherish the opportunity.

October 2, 2010

Only 23 weeks left until I get to see your beautiful face!! In about three weeks we find out if you're a boy or a girl. I am so excited!!!

Right now the debate in our home is where to put your baby bed. Our home is less than 800 square feet and we all sleep upstairs. Dad thinks you should sleep downstairs until you start sleeping through the night so you do not wake up him or James or Lauren. That means we need to figure out a baby bed for you. There's no room downstairs for a regular baby bed – even with the new addition Dad is building. Plus, it doesn't make sense for you to sleep downstairs when you nap because we'll all be downstairs making noise, doing school work, etc. So ... we are trying to figure out what to do. Any suggestions?

October 11, 2010

Sweet baby – every day is one day closer to seeing your beautiful face. We had a check-up today and all went well. You are exactly where you're supposed to be. And, I only gained one pound last month. That's pretty good considering how much I am eating! Pretty soon I'll be gaining more weight as you get bigger and bigger.

Dad noticed the other day how I always have my hand on my belly. I told him that's the only way I can hold you right now – just to let you know I am there! Next thing I know Dad's standing next to me with his hand on my belly – telling you he loves you, too.

October 14, 2010

Eleven more days until the big day! I can't wait! I think I've been feeling you kick every now and then. I feel a little twinge and then it's over. You are definitely getting bigger. My belly is growing a little every day. I can just feel it. My belly button is no longer an "inny" but is turning into an "outy." It seems earlier this time than with James or Lauren. But, alas, every pregnancy is different. Anyway, I just wanted to tell you that I love you and was thinking about you.

October 25, 2010

Here you are my beautiful baby girl! You're a girl!!! I can't believe it! We are going to be blessed with another daughter. Yeah!!

This is the halfway point in my pregnancy. Yeah! Maybe you'll be like James and Lauren and arrive early. This week I am going to pull out Lauren's baby clothes out and wash them for you. Everything will be all ready for your arrival. I can't wait!

I am feeling a lot better now. The morning sickness is officially gone. Although I am still ravenous, at least I am not getting sick! I was actually about to can apples this past weekend. Very cool!

November 5, 2010

Wow! You are definitely kicking up a storm these days! Dad was able to feel one of your kicks the other night. I love that feeling!

I think we may have come up with your first name: Caroline. It means "free person." Lauren was looking up girl names on the internet last night ... she even wrote down a list of ones she likes. So exciting!

November 10, 2010

Hello, sweet baby girl! This is week 22. We are more than halfway there! Pretty soon we'll get to meet you face to face. We've been steadily getting the house ready for your arrival. The little clothes saved from Lauren are all washed and ready. I bought the little screws, etc. to finish putting together your baby bed. I pick up your mattress on Friday. Dad has been working on finishing the new room. I think you and me will be sleeping in there for the first few months.

November 18, 2010

Sweet baby – you are doing so well! I feel your kicks get stronger every day. I am now at 23 weeks and feeling bigger every day. As you grow so do I!

Next week is Thanksgiving so we're finishing our lessons today and starting our holiday early! James and Lauren are excited to be out of school for an entire week! And I'll be glad for the rest!

I've been sick all this week. I think my congestion is almost gone but I still have a cough. I am hoping I'll be better by this weekend so we can go to Charlsye & Chris' home. We love visiting them (you will, too!).

We still haven't decided on your name. Caroline is still at the top of the list but we shall see! We still have some time before your arrival!

November 26, 2010

We celebrated Thanksgiving yesterday and what a beautiful day it turned out to be. I made our first Thanksgiving meal ever and it turned out to be an awesome meal – turkey, dressing, corn, mashed potatoes, green beans, homemade rolls, chocolate pie and apple pie. James made brownies and Lauren made chocolate chip cookies. Next year you'll get to partake in all the festivities. I did feel you kicking and moving around quite a bit last night.

I am now at 25 weeks. Yeah! In 15 weeks we should be meeting face to face. I am so excited about that! Your kicks are growing stronger every day. You're my miracle baby and I love you so very much.

We are still trying to put your baby bed together. I hope to finish that project this weekend. Dad finally finished the new room so now he can focus on the baby bed. Yeah!

December 6, 2010

Well, sweet baby girl – all is well with you. We see the midwife this Wednesday (in two days). I love going – simply so I can hear your heartbeat. It's a beautiful sound to my ears. You're kicking quite a bit these days. This morning it felt like you were doing rabbit punches! You're crazy!

We still haven't picked out a name for you. Here are a few Dad likes: Amanda Lynn and Amanda Danielle.

I am now at 26 weeks so we still have some time to decide. However, the really good news is that your bed is finally put together thanks to Dad. He had some time yesterday so he assembled it for you. I put a sheet on it and a blankie so it's all ready for you. Just a few more weeks and we'll be meeting each other face to face!

December 8, 2010
Twenty-seven weeks and counting! Not too much time left!

December 16, 2010
Yesterday was a pretty rough day ... at least for me. Monday I got a call from the clinic that I failed the glucose test from last week. So, yesterday I had to endure the three-hour glucose test. The problem was that I have such small veins they had many problems drawing blood. So, what should have been four pricks with a needle turned into eleven needle pricks! I had bandages all over my hands and arms. I am really praying that I pass this time. I do not want to have gestational diabetes. That would be awful! So, tomorrow we find out the results ... saying lots of prayers today.

December 20, 2010
The results are in and I don't have gestational diabetes. It was such awesome news!

We're getting ready for Christmas now. James and Lauren are pretty excited as we all are as Christmas approaches.

December 22, 2010
Three more days until Christmas! We'll be at Ma-Ma's and Pa-Pa's on Christmas Eve and Grandpa's on Christmas Day.

We finally finished all the shopping and will have all the presents under the tree very soon. Next year you'll be here for your first Christmas. That'll be so cool!

December 31, 2010
Thirty weeks! Only ten more weeks to go and you'll be here! We are busy preparing for your arrival. Lauren and I went and registered at Target – just in case anyone wants to buy you anything. Your bed is made and ready for you. Grandma is crocheting you a blanket. I have enough diapers and wipes to last around two months. Your stroller is in the back of the Tahoe and all your clothes are washed and folded – waiting for you to wear them.

You are definitely getting stronger as each week passes. Your kicks and stretches are bolder. Sometimes it feels like you're running a marathon!

We still haven't decided on your name yet. We're leaning towards Emma but that could change.

Love you bunches!

January 3, 2011

Cedar fever has hit our family with a vengeance. Dad's been sick since last week and the rest of us are in the midst of it. No fun! Right now my throat is scratchy, my head is stuffy and I am extremely tired. Maybe God's preparing us for your arrival (with the lack of sleep). I have a call with my boss Pam tonight and then I am off to bed.

You've been steadily kicking all night. Crazy girl! Dad came up with a new name tonight: Emma Blessing. That's what you are, you know?! You are our Blessing!

January 5, 2011

Today's appointment went very well. You are doing all that you need to be doing right now. I am now on a two-week appointment schedule for the next month and then we'll be down to once a week. It looks like I've only gained 16 pounds so far – that's great! You won't be a huge baby so that'll be good for delivery. I am not sure how much I gained with James and Lauren. I am just glad to know that all is well!

January 7, 2011

Today marks the beginning of the 31st week! Nine more weeks to go! Do you want to know the best news of all? We decided on your name! Are you ready? It's ... Emma Danielle Duke!!

Isn't that a beautiful name?! And so fitting – a little country with a Biblical twist since Danielle is a feminine form of Daniel.

Lauren got your bouncy thingy all cleaned up and in working order. You're a very blessed baby to have such a good big sister. James is excited, too. He just shows it differently (like rubbing my back or helping me get up or seeing if I need anything).

January 11, 2011

Darling, you've been pushing and kicking and running a marathon in my belly. Are you ready to come out? My back has been hurting quite a bit lately and you seem to have some body part lodged in my side down low ... not exactly comfortable!

I feel like a turtle on its back when I lay down - my arms and legs flailing around as I try to roll over to get up. I am sure I look like the picture of grace!

But, despite all this - you are definitely worth it ... no doubt about it. You need to stay inside a little bit longer until you're fully developed. I truly treasure this time with you. As this will probably be my last pregnancy, I am enjoying all that I can.

January 17, 2011

It's the beginning of the week and I am already tired! Hopefully I'll get more sleep tonight. Lauren's been coughing for the past three nights so I've been sleeping on the couch with Lauren. But, this is just a reminder of what's to come with you! I am sure you and I will be up many nights in the months to come.

January 20, 2011

Tomorrow will be 33 weeks. That means seven more weeks to go! This pregnancy seems to be both long and short. That's hard to understand I am sure - but sometimes I feel like I've been pregnant forever and then sometimes it feels like I've only been pregnant for a few weeks.

I am in the final stages of getting everything ready - both at work and at home. I am trying to get foods ready so that we can simply heat them up once you're born. I am sure I won't feel like cooking!

I can't wait to hold you in my arms and tell you how much I love you!

January 22, 2011

Last night I was sitting on the couch and all of a sudden I felt your hiccups! It's the first time you've had them. So cute! Dad didn't think you could have the hiccups in the womb - but after feeling them he's now a believer.

Also, we got our first baby gift last night from Pam, Nichole and Connie. It was a baby food maker, spoons, a cookbook and storage containers. Talk about exciting! I am about halfway through the cookbook! It's so awesome - all so I can make your baby food. I think that's just too cool!

January 30, 2011

Yesterday Charlsye and I went to a baby shower for our cousin, Jenna. Her baby (also your cousin) is due the week before you. The crazy thing is if their baby is a girl, her name will also be Emma! They are waiting until their baby is delivered to find out if it's a boy or a girl. But, if it's a boy, his name will be Cole. Kinda cool! It would be really cool if y'all were born on the same day and you were both girls named Emma! That would be awesome.

The other night we were blessed with a high chair from David and Christina. It can also convert to a rocking horse or a desk. It's a beautiful high chair and I am so thankful that they thought of us to give it to. They're really good people.

As for you and me, we're doing great. You still kick like crazy and we're all very excited to hold and meet you!

February 1, 2011

Wow! We've been battin' down the hatches today. An arctic cold front is ramming its way through the states. We've seen a few snow flurries today but there are more expected on Thursday night (in two days). When we went to the midwife appointment today there were three women in labor and at least one or two more headed to the South location! With the arrival of the cold front it sent them into labor. But, all is well with us. My blood pressure was a little lower than normal but everything else was fine. Just two more weeks and you'll be considered "mature" which means that if you were born at 36 weeks you'd be just fine.

February 6, 2011

It's hard to believe that we're already into February! Five more weeks (somewhere in there) and you'll be making your grand appearance. Sometimes I still can't believe that God has granted and blessed us with another child. Had my first pregnancy not ended in miscarriage, we would have four beautiful children. But, we will have three blessings here on earth and one day I'll get to meet my other baby in heaven.

God has plans for you, Emma. You're one of His children. He will guide your steps and lead you on a grand adventure in this life. Stay true to Him and you will be blessed. Life has its ups and downs but just remember that God is always in control and you can lean on Him when times are tough.

I never thought I would have another child – but God can work miracles and you are our miracle baby. I thank God every day for my beautiful family – Dad, James, Lauren and you, Emma. Welcome to our family. We all look forward to kissing your cheeks.

February 14, 2011
Happy Valentine's Day, Emma! Even though you haven't made your grand debut just yet – know that you are definitely very much loved! Dad was the first one to tell you Happy Valentine's Day. He beat me to the punch!

We are on countdown mode! Only four weeks left and counting. I am so ready to see you and give you all kinds of hugs and kisses (so is Dad!).

The only thing we have left to do is fix the glider. We got the car seat yesterday so I'll probably get it installed in the Tahoe tonight or tomorrow. I want to be ready for your arrival!

You'll be here before we know it!

February 15, 2011
I met with Roswitha today – one of the midwives. What a nice woman! She said that your head is definitely down more towards the pelvis – which I understand means that you've dropped. Yeah! You've been measuring right on with how far along I am (as far as weeks) but now you're measuring at 35 weeks. Roswitha thinks that may be because you've dropped. She also thinks you might weigh around 5.5 pounds right now. If you continue with the same weight gain you'll be around 7.5 pounds in four weeks. That's a good weight! So, just stay in there as long as you can, Emma! But, all is well so far. She said all my numbers look good and that I've only gained 24 pounds. Very cool!

February 20, 2011
Well, sweetie – three weeks and counting! It's a hard to believe this pregnancy is almost over and we'll finally get to meet each other – face-to-face, cheek-to-cheek and heart-to-heart.

I am not looking forward to the pain but know through pain you will make your grand entrance into this crazy world.

I've been having problems sleeping over the last few days. I toss and turn from around 3:30 a.m. on. I guess I am preparing for those long nights that are coming!

Dad has been pretty worried lately – making sure that I am resting and not overdoing anything. He said he got emotional the other day about meeting you. He's definitely pretty excited!

February 22, 2011

Okey dokey, sweetie. We're at 37 weeks and counting! Our appointment went very well today. I am so ready for you to come out!!! We're so close and yet it seems like you'll never get here!

February 26, 2011

Thirteen days until your due date! Right now we're fishing in Salado. We spent the day running errands all over Georgetown and we're ending it by doing a little fishing. Well, I am relaxing and getting ready to start reading but Dad, Lauren and James are all fishing. One of these days you'll be sitting on the bank with me watching them fish (at least until you're old enough to hold a pole).

I am really feeling huge right now. I've only gained 25-26 pounds but my lower back is killing me and somehow I twisted the top part of my ankle. I have no idea how I did that. Every slight pain or move and I think labor is starting but not yet. Maybe you'll be early like James and Lauren or you could be right on time. I am really not looking forward to thinking you might be late. But, only you and God know when you'll arrive.

March 1, 2011

You could literally be born any day now. We thought I might have been in labor last night but after a few hours the contractions stopped. At my appointment today the midwife said that all looks good. It seems your head is still down but you are now facing the other direction – which would explain a lot of the strange movements I felt within the last week.

Today I am baking a pineapple upside down cake and snicker doodles for Dad. My hope is that all this movement will get labor going soon.

March 2, 2011

I am not feeling so well today. My eyes are watering. My throat is scratchy – not to mention my head hurts and my nose is runny. There must be something in the air causing my sinuses and allergies to act up. No fun! I really want to be at my best when I go into labor. I am praying that God will make me better before then!

March 5, 2011

All righty – we're at 39 weeks ... and I am still waiting. I've been real moody today. I still have the cold, my back hurts awfully bad and I am tired. I really want to see you and hold you and give you lots of kisses. But, I am still waiting. Are you negotiating with God to stay longer? I know it's truly all in His timing. I just need to be more patient.

March 8, 2011

Dilated to 2-3 centimeters
Effaced: 50%
Station: -1
Emma's heartbeat: 152 bpm

Roswitha said I have a cute belly (too funny!). Could be any day or next week. Come on Emma!!

March 13, 2011

My dear, sweet Emma, you will always be in my heart. Always! I went into labor at 8 p.m. on Thursday, March 10th. All day, though, I'd been trying to get you to move, but I never felt you move once that day. Dad thought that you might be sleeping. I should have called the birthing center but I didn't. I thought you might be sleeping as well.

By the time I called the midwife to go in it was around 1:15 a.m. on Friday, March 11th. We met at the birthing center but Charlotte could not find your heartbeat. We tried all kinds of techniques and positions but nothing. We even tried an ultrasound but still couldn't find your heartbeat. Charlotte suggested we go to the hospital. We followed her there and after more searches with a fetal heart monitor and two doctors tried an ultrasound but they confirmed our worst nightmare – there was no heartbeat. You had already passed away.

I couldn't understand why my miracle baby had died before she was even born. How were we supposed to plan a funeral for a baby who hadn't even been born yet? All our hopes and dreams for you died that day. Dad and I clung to each other while the doctors determined the best course to take. Deep sobs racked my body. I remember how lost I felt.

But through it all, a peace came over us. God had a plan for you, Emma. It wasn't in His plan for you to be with us, but to go home to glory. It broke our hearts to let you go, but God's plan superseded ours.

You were born at 8:18 a.m. after three pushes. From the time I was given the epidural and petocin, it was only 30-45 minutes that you were delivered. Dad was as strong as ever. "You're doing great. You can do it." It was so sad and so quiet when you were born. The doctor had to stitch me up and clean up, but the nurse took you and gave you a bath so we could hold you. The doctor said I was bleeding too much so they had to give me a shot to slow it down. Dad was very nervous. He said he couldn't lose both you and me. It would have been too much for him.

We had so many people come by that day to pay their respects to you and us. It was so heartwarming to have so much support. We rocked you, sang you lullabies, held you, kissed you, rubbed your feet (which were so soft) and messed up your hair. You are so loved and we miss you so very much. My heart still aches for you and I long to hold you in my arms and caress your little cheeks with soft kisses.

Even now Dad says our home is too quiet. He was looking forward to those long nights helping you go back to sleep. It's almost eerie how quiet the nights are. Your empty bed breaks my heart. You should be sleeping in it.

But, I know that you're in a better place. I truly believe that. It's for my own selfish reasons that I want you here with me.

Last night I remembered that early in my pregnancy I dedicated you to God as a thank you for His blessing us with you. There is a story in the Bible of a mother (Hannah) who did the same thing with her son and he grew up to be a great prophet (Samuel). Little did I know that God planned a glorious road for you - even before you were born. I'd dedicate you to Him again if given the chance. Yes, my heart is broken. Yes, my dreams for you crumbled. But, you are our angel now resting in Jesus' arms. What a joy for a mother!

March 14, 2011

My sweet Emma - my heart aches. I miss you so much. I wish I could hold you in my arms, sing you lullabies as I rock you to sleep and smother you with kisses. It's been three days since you've gone to heaven and it already feels like a lifetime. I want to nurse you and wake up with you in the middle of the night. I want to hear your laugh and see your pretty smile. I'd love to know what color your eyes would have been. I cling to your dad and hold him tight while we both grieve your death. Our loss is heaven's gain. Jesus rocks you for me. You'll never be hungry or know pain or sorrow. You're in the best care of all. I know that one day we'll be together again and I can't wait to hold you in my arms once more. Just know that I love you and I miss you like I've never missed anyone ever before. I see our pictures of you and wish I could go back and hold you once more – feel your soft hair and rub the bottoms of your feet. I've never known a pain so deep. It rocks me to the core ... brings me to my knees. But, I pray and ask for God's strength and He provides it in my hour of need. He loves you. I love you and with God's help I know Dad and I will make it through this sorrow. You are my sunshine, Emma Danielle. Shine on, shine on, shine on ...

March 19, 2011

Your funeral was March 18th and what a joyous ceremony it was. Brother Dan, Phil and Barry sang *I'll Fly Away* acapella. It was no funeral dirge but a joyous celebration of where you are! Then we all sang *This Little Light of Mine*. Brother Dan read the eulogy that Dad and I wrote for you. He finished with a message about how much God loves children. He even told the story of how shepherds will send a ewe or lamb across a river to get the rest of the flock to cross. If the little one can make it then it doesn't seem so difficult for the others. You are our little lamb crossing over into heaven. I really look forward to going there so we can meet face-to-face and I can hold you once more.

I miss you. Dad misses you. We love you very much. Shine on, sweet Emma, shine on!

Emma's Eulogy
March 11, 2011

March 11th is a day that most will remember as the day Japan was hit with an earthquake, a tsunami and nuclear reactor problems. But back here in Austin, Texas, our own little world was literally shaken to its foundations. Our little Emma came into this world in a way so unexpected and so heartbreaking that no one was prepared for the heart-crushing words, "I am sorry, but she has no heartbeat." There's no way to explain the feeling of despair and sorrow that those words had on us. Our hopes and dreams of a bigger family were dissolved in a matter of mere seconds – no midnight feedings or dances around the house to calm baby Emma. The diapers would never be used, the car seat would never hold little Emma and we would leave the hospital with no baby in our arms. We wondered, "How do we plan a funeral for a baby who hasn't even been born yet?"

However, in the midst of the fire, a sudden and unexplained peace came into our lives – a peace that surpasses all understanding. From the moment those words were uttered, our lives were forever changed and so were those around us. Hearts opened that had been closed and unreachable. God's grace filled the room almost instantly - a grace so strong only an angel could have prompted our Father in heaven to fill the room with his spirit. Emma was that angel - pleading for her parents and everyone else involved.

I can tell all of you here, and a lot of you were in the room with us at one point or another, that something God-inspired happened that day. A force from our Almighty God moved around the room, setting a tone of love, peace, and understanding that can only come from Heaven. Men of the strongest steel were left as weak as a newborn babe. Women hardened by life became supple and malleable again. Questions about life, eternity and heaven were raised again and again. How could this happen? Why did it have to be Emma? People not sure of their faith suddenly had clarity and vision. We often said this baby was our miracle baby – but the miracle of Emma was not in her life, but in her passing on to heaven. Had she lived, we would not have seen God's mercy, love, grace, forgiveness and peace enter so many lives. Emma's passing made people face the world and the reality of life and death. She made people dare to be strong, to walk the line, to profess their faith. We were able to laugh and cry over our sweet Emma. Complete strangers were made Brothers and Sisters in Christ our Lord.

Emma came with a message from God. She wanted to let everyone know that everything is going to be ok. God has us cradled in His everlasting arms. She wanted everyone to know that laughter is the best medicine for the soul. We're joyful that Emma is in heaven with Jesus – where He wants us all to be. She wanted everyone to be the best they can be for all things should done for the glory of God. Parents - hug your children, young or old. They are blessings from God and should be treated as treasures. Worldly possessions don't really matter. Lay your treasures up in heaven for earthly possessions will rust or decay. And most of all she wanted to remind people that they should turn on their lights. She's probably giggling as she sees the looks on your faces right about now, but she said, "Make sure they turn the light up all the way." Let your light shine everywhere you go. Be a light to the world so that others may know Christ. Through her passing, Emma had an ability to bring people together. She had the amazing grace only angels have. Emma Danielle wants you to know she loves all of you and she wants you to know that Jesus loves you, too.

And we wanted to tell Emma – we love you so much and we look forward to the day that we can meet you face to face in heaven, where we can laugh with you, pick flowers in the clouds, slide down rainbows and give you all the hugs and kisses we'll have stored up for you while here on earth. Jesus holds you now and we know that there's no better place for you to be. We'll see your smile in every sunbeam and know that you're smiling back at us. Shine on, sweet Emma, shine on.

The Message at Emma's Funeral
by Dan Wooldridge, Sr. Pastor at Crestview Baptist Church

I stood this last Sunday here in two services with large numbers of people in both services and shared with them that I was blessed, moved and touched by the faith that John and Meredith showed in Christ by the strength that the Holy Spirit was providing for them in the face of what they had to work and deal with, with the passing of little Emma Danielle.

I've been blessed in every exchange by telephone or by email or even with the writing of this eulogy that I just shared with you. I have been a pastor for nearly forty years. I have worked with families in every imaginable situation. John and Meredith, I have never worked with a couple who had to face what you're facing and who handled it better, more beautifully and with a greater commitment to honor God - not to be bitter but to glorify Him and trust Him - than you have. I commend you again as I did Sunday for what I already observed in your life. The Bible says we walk by faith and not by sight and Christians have to believe things that they cannot see.

I was thinking about 2 Samuel 12:23. King David (who of all the characters in the Word of God certainly is one of the more important, an ancestor of Jesus Christ, humanly speaking) lost a young child, prayed earnestly and fasted, but finally said, "I shall go to him but he shall not return to me." That fits today, doesn't it? I shall go to her but she shall not return to me. That acceptance, faith, and awareness of God's promises in those simple words of King David, I have seen and heard from you as well. I absolutely agree that amazingly trials like this can be turned into a triumph. They can elevate our consciousness to the value and preciousness of life. They can greatly increase our awareness of the life beyond.

I was told a long time ago by shepherds that if you're trying to get sheep to cross a fast-moving stream that one of the best things you can do is get a ewe, or maybe even a lamb, across the water. Once one of them has crossed, the rest lose their fear and follow.

There's something about knowing that someone so dear, loved and anticipated is in glory that takes the fear of it away. The fear of the unknown, that creates in us a consciousness, a hunger, and a desire that all people can know the peace that passes all understanding that you testified to. The apostle Paul talked about that as a byproduct of a relationship with Jesus Christ. He said that for those of us who live in faith and in prayer, a peace that passes all understanding will keep our hearts and our minds through Jesus Christ. I've seen that in your lives.

I couldn't help but think also about a passage in the Gospel of Mark (Mark 10:13-16). Some might say, "Where do you get this idea that there is life beyond and that Emma Danielle is there – conscious, aware and very much alive?" People were bringing little children to Jesus to have Him touch them but the disciples rebuked them. When Jesus saw this He was indignant. That means He was angry. I've often said, do you want to know what makes Jesus angry? It makes Jesus angry when we get in the way of and hinder children from having free, unfettered access to the Lord. And then He said, "Let the little children come to me and do not hinder them for the kingdom of God belongs to such as these." It's obvious that these children couldn't have explained who Jesus was or why He came. They were not theologians. They were just children. And yet, Jesus said this is exactly the kind of people that He came to produce. He said, "I tell you the truth, anyone who will not receive the kingdom of God like a little child will never enter it." But let us not leave out this verse. It's the sixteenth in Mark 10, "And he took the children in His arms, put his hands on them and blessed them."

We believe that Emma Danielle is with the Lord because we know that life begins at conception. We believe that she's with the Lord because everything that He said then is still true today. His Word abides forever. We know that the Word teaches us there is an innocent stage when our children are unborn or even small or young, in which they are in a relationship with God. I spend a lot of time working with children and always have. I must tell you that children have a natural trust in God. It's just easy for them. They may ask some questions that cause you to scratch your head trying to come up with an answer, but it is obvious what Jesus was saying. He was saying the kingdom of God belongs to such as these and unless you become like them in your faith and in your trust, you will never enter the kingdom of God.

I am beginning a series of messages this Sunday about the life beyond. One of the stories that I will be telling in the course of that series is about a young boy named Colton Burpo, who had a ruptured appendix and apparently died in the emergency care that he was receiving. But, as so often happens in our day, he was revived.

In the course of his story Colton tells what he experienced in those moments. He looked at his mom one day, who was standing there and he said, "Mom, I have a sister, don't I?" He wasn't talking about the sister who was alive and in the house. He was talking about the sister who had died before birth, a sister they had never told Colton about. He said he saw her and she wasn't a baby. She had a maturity. She was still young but she had a maturity about her. Colton said he soon realized that she was his sister. He also identified a relative from a picture he had seen. If that were just an isolated incident in a child's imagination we could all be skeptical, but there are hundreds of thousands of such stories from literally around the world in every nation on the planet with people who have had near death experiences and encounters difficult for them to explain.

We don't base our faith on Colton Burpo's story. We base our faith on the Word of God. Once Jesus was looking into the troubled faces of His disciples and He said these words, "Let not your heart be troubled; you believe in God, believe also in Me. In My Father's house are many mansions; if it were not so, I would have told you. I go to prepare a place for you. And if I go and prepare a place for you, I will come again and receive you to Myself; that where I am, there you may be also. And where I go you know, and the way you know." Thomas, whom we sometimes call Doubting Thomas, interrupted Jesus and said, "Lord, we don't know where you're going and how can we know the way?" I am glad he interrupted Jesus because then Jesus said, "I am the way, the truth and the life. No one comes to the Father except through me" (John 14:1-6).

How is it possible to rejoice, to laugh, to not be bitter on a day like today? The same way that Jesus was speaking of that day when you have a rock solid faith in Jesus Christ, when you know that His life was a sinless life and His death was an atoning death. That simply means that He died for us. He died so that we who don't pass as children in our innocence could nevertheless be forgiven and find entry into glory. Do what He said when He spoke about the children that day. Be converted and become like a little child – to have the kind of change that allows us to trust implicitly and completely. Jesus simply said to them, "I am the way, the truth and the life." In other words, everybody that goes into heaven goes through Christ, even Emma Danielle, but certainly those who put their trust in Jesus can find in Him a way and a glory.

But you know what He said more in those verses? I am going to prepare a place for you and in order to deal with a day like today you have to believe that heaven is real. By the way, Colton Burpo, with the help of his father and some others, has written a book about his experience and that's the title, *Heaven is for Real*. You have to know that heaven is not just some dream that people have, some way of dealing with our struggles and sorrows but that there truly is a place like Jesus spoke of in glory. In fact, once in a prayer, Jesus longingly spoke about being in glory again. He said, "Glorify me to the Father in heaven with your own self, with the glory that I had with you before the world was" (John 17:5). What an amazing prayer that was. However wonderful you think heaven is - it's more than that. And Jesus simply said to those troubled people that day, "Don't worry. There's a place." But also, if you notice, there's the promise: I will come again.

It might have seemed odd to some of you for us to begin this afternoon singing, "I'll Fly Away." It always is a little strange when people don't really know the Word of God. That song is about the fact that one day everything that's wrong with this world will be done away. There will be a day when we move beyond this place and its problems and into glory. The passage of scripture that teaches us this is what Jesus said: "I will come again." What He's saying to us is the same that is said in Revelation 21 that He would wipe away every tear from our eyes and there would be no more death, neither sickness, sorrow nor crying and neither shall there be any more pain, for the former things will have passed away.

Maybe some of you have heard of C.S. Lewis. He loved to write children's stories. *The Chronicles of Narnia* are his. He also was a great Christian. C.S. Lewis talked a great deal about what we should expect when we stand before God in heaven. One of the things that he said is especially important today: "I believe someday that we'll stand before God in heaven and we'll say over and over, 'Ah! Now I understand ... Now I understand.'" It's very normal to ask questions about why this had to be. With all the confidence I have in the Lord I am absolutely certain that nothing has changed about His love for Emma Danielle or this family. There will even be a day when all the mysteries will be clear, every question answered and every tear wiped from every eye. That's what the promise means: "I will come again." Emma is in a wonderful place, receiving the best that God has to offer.

What about us? If you listened carefully to that eulogy a while ago you should know that John and Meredith want me to say to you that the hope we have in glory is through personal faith in Jesus Christ. How does that happen? What brings us to that place where as Jesus said we can be converted like a little child so that we'll enter into heaven? Not a little child in the fact that we go back to the limited understanding that a child has but a child in the sense that our heart is clean before God. How does that happen? First we have to realize that God really loves us. God loves you. God loves everyone in this room no matter where you've been or whatever you've done. God loves you. We also have to realize that in time, through the course of our lives, we are separated from God by sin. We can argue that but the fact is that a barrier is erected between us. Isaiah the prophet said it this way, "Our sins have separated between us and our God and they have hidden His face from us" (Isaiah 59:2).

Do you ever notice that the things that were delightful when you were a little child are not quite as big a deal later? Do you know why that is? It's because the world kind of takes away the glow. Sin separates us from God. And sin, don't stumble over that word, means that we've missed the purpose for which God created us. Now, it has many applications but what it means at its core is that God has a purpose for every one of our lives and we miss it. The word literally means to miss the mark. But you know Jesus didn't miss the mark. Every minute of every day of His life Jesus was in the center of the perfect will of God. He lived a completely sinless life. Because He did, Jesus could take my sin upon Himself and die for my sin on the cross.

When the time came and I understood the good news of Jesus, I could find forgiveness and release, be converted and become like a child by inviting Jesus Christ to come and live in my life by faith. I did that a long time ago. In John 1:12, he said, "As many as received Him (that's Jesus) to them He gave the power to become the children of God." Do you remember what Jesus said? Unless you become like a little child you will not enter the kingdom of heaven. As many as received Jesus into their heart by faith, to them He gave the power to become the children of God. There's that word again, children. By receiving Jesus Christ into our hearts by faith we can become like a little child. I hope you've done that.

Long ago I prayed, God, thank you for loving me. I know I've sinned and I need your forgiveness. Jesus, thank you for dying on the cross for me. Come into my life and be my Lord. Help me to be the person you want me to be. And He came. The greatest thing that would happen from Emma's passing is what has already happened – John and Meredith would have a greater boldness to speak about the Lord Jesus and to share the love of the Lord Jesus with others. Get ready. They're not going to be timid about it any more. The second great thing that could happen is that anyone in this room who is not at peace with God would come to know the peace that passes understanding through a personal relationship with Jesus Christ. If you desire that and don't have it, ask about it. Let it be known that you want to talk about it. Johnny can talk with you about it. I can talk with you about it. Don't let it slide. It's too important.

Let's pray. Father, your promises are so wonderful and so real. We thank you, God, for the assurances. We couldn't deal with life, much less death, if it weren't for the promises of Your Word. Through Your Word, Lord, there is hope and even joy! Lord, I pray that Emma's coming to be with you will be the occasion of many coming to be with You - by whatever means or whatever process that You choose to use – whether that is through the witness of John and Meredith, their children, or the moments we've shared today. God, just through the way You take our trials and our tragedies and turn them into triumphs. Lord, may the grace that You have shown us and the comfort Your Word promises to be with all here present. In the name of Jesus, Amen.

Part II

Reflections

Chapter 5
God's Plan for You

For I know the thoughts that I think toward you, says the Lord, thoughts of peace and not of evil, to give you a future and a hope. – Jeremiah 29:11

As I mentioned before, our first night in the hospital was a long one. Johnny and I had not slept since Thursday morning. Emma was born at 8:18 Friday morning and from that point on we had visitors nonstop in the hospital room until late Friday night. We were exhausted mentally, physically and emotionally. By that point, Johnny had a migraine so we were trying to make him comfortable and help his headache go away. It was not very easy to get comfortable and fall asleep, though. Earlier that evening the nurse had finally removed all my physical ties to the machines, but I couldn't find a comfortable position as my body ached, my mind was still a whirlwind of thoughts, and my emotions were either grieving at our loss of Emma or joyous about Emma being in heaven. I cried or laughed at any given moment.

Despite all the chaos of the day and our exhaustion, Johnny and I were talking about the peace that surrounded us. When Johnny's headache had gone, I was lying in the hospital bed in complete stillness, finally resting. But in that stillness, I heard a soft voice, *"I know the plans I have for you."* Those are the only words I heard but I knew instantly and without a doubt that it was God. When we are moving, struggling, talking, listening to music, playing games or chatting with friends we cannot hear the Lord when He speaks. Sometimes I'll get a knock on the head and realize He's trying to get my attention, but that night I was taken back to Psalm 46:10, "Be still and know that I am God." It is in our quiet moments that we can hear Him. It is not always a booming voice, but sometimes a quiet, tender voice, a voice full of love and concern – a voice with a message. His message came through that night in the stillness of the room and the quietness of my thoughts. And my answer? Okay, Lord, show me what you want me to do. Lead me and I will follow.

As I write this, it has only been a few months since Emma went to heaven. His promise still holds true today as it did back in the hospital. I am still waiting on Him, asking daily what it is that He wants me to do. In the meantime, I am reading His Word and walking on the water with Jesus. I do not know how we will pay the bills this month, but I know they will be paid somehow because God will provide. We are taking everything one day at a time - no more, no less. He's taken care of me through all these years and seen to all my needs and those of my family. He won't stop now.

No Work + No Money = God's Perfect Timing

Johnny and I worked for the same small company. For about two-and-a-half years Johnny was the property manager for three of the owners' buildings. This was no small fete. The company owners' home itself was pristine with two acres of flowers, lush grass, an intricate sprinkler system and it all required regular maintenance, trimming, weeding, mowing and planting. The property is so beautiful it could be featured in a magazine. That is not including the same plants and maintenance required at one of the commercial properties.

After Emma passed away, the company left my position open to see if I had an interest in returning. I remember asking Johnny at the hospital, "Do I have to go back now?" Johnny quickly answered, "Not if you don't want to." Good. We were still on the same page. Although I appreciated the thought, I knew in my heart that God still wanted me to be at home, full time, not working at all (at least on anything outside of the home).

On the heels of losing Emma and returning to work, life had a completely new perspective for both of us. The things that were once so important took a backseat to what we felt God was calling us to do. My focus was more directed towards our home life and being a stay-at-home mom and Johnny becoming the sole financial provider for the family. Our income was reduced by half. In 2006 Johnny became a licensed real estate agent and split his time between that and handling the property management of the residence and commercial buildings of our bosses. Even though the property management job was paying the bills every month, it took away from his real estate business, which was suffering. Luke 16:13 says, "No servant can serve two masters; for either he will hate the one and love the other, or else he will be loyal to the one and despise the other. You cannot serve God and mammon." This verse still holds true today. We were making just enough to get by, but not enough to put back and save or get ahead and it was wearing on Johnny going from one to the other.

Johnny made the decision to quit both and go back into sales with an established company due to the looming medical bills and the general expense of living each month. He explained this to the owners and within two weeks he was out of work as they replaced him with another contractor. Less than three months after Emma was born, we were both out of work with only about a thousand dollars in the bank. For a few days we were both frustrated and angry, but came to realize that God had a different plan for us. The door to our old way of life was completely shut. This was the first time in thirteen years that we were not connected to this company. This was another reminder that although we think we are in control, we are not (but God is).

Although Johnny had an interview or two, he did not have any job offers. For several weeks afterward we made ends meet purely by God's grace. We sold what we could on E-bay and my husband started really diving into real estate to see if it would pick up. In the meantime, he started giving bids for handyman work but his bids were not selected. The one bid he did get ended up falling through before we even started on it. While we thought that this was what God wanted us to do, it turned out not to be so.

While we waited on God for answers and direction, we devoted more time to Him and felt the need to start serving Him. Our first serving experience was volunteering for Camp Crestview, a full 8-hour day, week-long Vacation Bible School. It was just what we needed. We saw many children accept Christ, including our son, James, who was baptized a month later.

This is also when I started selling baked goods (pies, breads, and jams) to help make ends meet until God opened doors for Johnny.

Despite these hurdles and discouragement, we continued to stand on God's Word and our faith. While we may not always understand His plans, they are still superior to ours.

God's Plan for You

God has a plan for you, too. You were designed and created for some great work, something that God has in mind that only you can do. I do not know what that is. You may not even know what it is ... yet. But the Lord does. He will tell you when He is ready for you to know – when He feels you are ready, and when you are listening and obeying Him. In the meantime, bloom where you are planted. Trust in the Lord with all your heart, and lean not on your own understanding (Proverbs 3:5).

I love the scene in the movie, *Facing the Giants*[4], where Mr. Bridges tells Coach Taylor that the Lord is not finished with Him yet and he still has an open door at the school and until the Lord moves him he is to bloom right where he is planted. From Revelation 3:8 he quotes, "I know your works. See, I have set before you an open door, and no one can shut it; for you have a little strength, have kept My word, and have not denied My name."

Mr. Bridges then tells the story of two farmers who both needed and prayed for rain. One farmer went out to prepare his fields for rain and the other one did not. Mr. Bridges asked, "Which one do you think trusted God to send the rain? Which farmer are you? God will send the rain when He's ready. Are you prepared to receive it when the rain comes? Are you prepared for what God has in store for you?" God is preparing you, just as He's preparing me and Johnny. You may not be ready and there may be other trials that you must weather in order to be ready.

Pastor Paul Sheppard is the founder of Destiny Christian Fellowship. I love listening to his sermons. Johnny and I were listening to Pastor's Paul sermon, "It was God,"[5] on a podcast one night. He was speaking about testimonies and messages and that you cannot have a "test-i-mony" without a TEST. It (the word "test") is at the very beginning of the word. And, you cannot have a message without a MESS. You must get through the TEST and the MESS before you can have a testimony or a message. He equates it to someone who has never had children giving parental advice or a single person (who has never been married) giving marital advice. God wants us to be a blessing to others who may be going through something similar. If you have lived through it, suffered through it, leaned on God through it, then you can bless others with your personal insight. We have all been through difficulties in life whether it is divorce, bankruptcy, marital infidelity, the loss of a child, drug addiction, alcoholism, etc. The list can go on and on.

There is a purpose to all that happens in life. There are no coincidences. Yes, some of it is through our own doing (like Saul in the New Testament), and sometimes it is not (like Joseph in the Old

---

[4] Facing the Giants. DVD. Sherwood Baptist Church of Albany Georgia, Inc. 2006
[5] The sermon is available for purchase through Pastor Paul's website: http://www.pastorpaul.net. You can also click this link to purchase it: http://shop.pastorpaul.net/It-Was-God-1109.htm?categoryId=-1

Testament) but regardless, God will use you or your circumstances for His plan.

There was nothing I did that caused Emma to die. The cord was wrapped around her neck three times. The doctor believed she died approximately twenty-four hours before she was born (based on her skin condition at the time of delivery). I can either be angry with God or understand that there was a higher purpose. The Lord is calling me to do something else and by living through and experiencing grief through Emma's death, I can be a blessing to someone else who may be experiencing the same issue. Or, perhaps you have been through alcoholism and have come out as a champion on the other side. God can take a devastating situation and turn it into a blessing – maybe not now, maybe not next year, but one day He'll be able to use you as a blessing to someone else. Romans 8:28 says that "all things work together for good to those who love God, to those who are the called according to His purpose." Or, sometimes God uses a situation to glorify Himself, such as the healing of the blind man in John 9 (verses 1-3). The disciples asked Jesus if the man or his parents sinned, which caused his blindness. Jesus answered, "Neither this man nor his parents sinned, but that the works of God should be revealed in him." God used Jesus to heal the blind man, simply to show the power of God. It is through His glory that others can come into His kingdom.

Think about Saul (aka Paul) in the New Testament. Saul hated Christians. He hated the new church that was springing up all over Jerusalem, Bethlehem and throughout the rest of the Roman Empire following Jesus' death and resurrection. Saul was even there for the stoning of the first martyr, Stephen. He despised the early Christians and wanted to destroy them and the church, even going so far as to pull men and women from their homes and throw them into jail (Acts 8:3). However, God had other plans for Saul. He was on his way to Damascus when a light shone around him and he heard Jesus asking him, "Saul, Saul, why are you persecuting me?" He put scales over Saul's eyes and when the scales were removed several days later, Paul (as he was later called) became the greatest advocate of the church, writing many of the books and letters in the New Testament. Paul was called to a higher purpose despite his initial ill will towards Christians and Christ. Jesus took a persecutor and turned him into a believer who brought others to Christ.

Consider Joseph from the Old Testament (Genesis 37) who was sold into slavery by his brothers who hated him. Joseph worked his way up through the ranks at Potipher's home and was then tossed into jail when he refused an illicit affair with Potipher's wife (who actually accused him of rape). But, because God was with him, Joseph eventually earned his way up to the second highest ranking position in the Egyptian empire, answering only to the pharaoh himself. By doing so, he was able to bring his father, Jacob, and all the rest of his family into Egypt and therefore save future generations of God's chosen people (the Israelites). Because God is all-knowing and all-powerful, thousands of men, women and children were saved from starvation due to Joseph's dreams and the fulfillment of those dreams by God.

The situations occurred despite what circumstances were created by these men (Saul persecuting Christians) or simply happened to them (Joseph being thrown into the well and sold into slavery). Both of these examples show that God can use all things for good for those who love Him (Romans 8:28) and His works can be glorified in the process (John 9:1-3).

As a mother I can bless other new moms with my experiences in pregnancy, labor, delivery, post-recovery, breastfeeding, or I can simply be an ear for venting or lend a shoulder for tears. I have "been there" and "done that."

As a mother of a stillborn (and also having miscarried), I can now also offer comfort in this area. Death is difficult and grieving is painful, but there is light at the end of the tunnel (and that light is God).

Chapter 6
Lessons Learned

Let us therefore come boldly to the throne of grace, that we may obtain mercy and find grace to help in time of need.
Hebrews 4:16

Through all the emotional tidal waves I went through and even up until now, I am learning from Emma and her death. Here are some of the lessons I have learned so far:

Pray

Prayer is the most important way to communicate with God. Through prayer God listens to what we lift up to Him (i.e., our own concerns and issues, prayers for others, or praise for God). It is also our opportunity to listen to what God may be telling us. In essence, it is a conversation between you and God. He not only listens to what we verbally say, but also to those silent prayers on our heart. These quiet, inward prayers, the ones we do not know what to say or how to voice, are carried up to God through the Holy Spirit, who intercedes for us "with groanings that cannot be uttered" (Romans 8:26). Psalm 34:17 says that "The righteous cry out, and the Lord hears, and delivers them out of all their troubles." God hears all, knows all and sees all. He hears the prayers we say and knows those we are afraid to voice – those prayers that the Holy Spirit groans for us.

In the Old Testament, two women in particular who prayed for children were Rachel (Joseph's mother) and Hannah (the mother of Samuel, the prophet).

Jacob was in love with Rachel, who had an older sister named Leah. Jacob and his father-in-law, Laban, struck a deal. Jacob would work for Laban seven years in exchange for Rachel's hand in marriage. But on the wedding day Laban pulled a little bit of trickery and switched brides, causing Jacob to marry the oldest daughter, Leah! Jacob confronted Laban, who said that his oldest daughter must marry. Jacob agreed to work another seven years for Rachel. After Jacob married both ladies, the race for children was on between Rachel and Leah. Leah conceived and bore six sons and one daughter before Rachel even had one child. There was animosity among the sisters (wives). Leah wanted Jacob to love her as he loved Rachel and Rachel wanted to bear Jacob sons as Leah was able to do. Genesis 30:22 says, "Then God remembered Rachel, and God listened to her and opened her womb." How does God listen to us? Through prayer.

Hannah's story is similar to Rachel's. Elkanah had two wives, Peninnah and Hannah. 1 Samuel 1:2 says that Peninnah already had children but that Hannah had none. When Elkanah would make his annual sacrifice to the Lord "he would give portions to Peninnah his wife" but to Hannah "he would give a double portion, for he loved Hannah, although the LORD had closed her womb" (1 Samuel 1:4-5). Every year Hannah would pray and weep over the children she did not have. Finally, she made a vow to God, "O Lord of hosts, if You will indeed look on the affliction of Your maidservant and remember me, and not forget Your maidservant, but will give Your maidservant a male child, then I will give him to the Lord all the days of his life, and no razor shall come upon his head" (1 Samuel 1:11). Shortly following her vow and the blessing of the high priest, Eli, Hannah lay with Elkanah and conceived a son. When she delivered him she named her son, Samuel, and once he was weaned, she took him back to the high priest and dedicated him to the Lord saying, "I prayed for this child, and the Lord has granted me what I asked of him. So now I give him to the Lord. For his whole life he will be given over to the Lord." Samuel went on to become a great prophet.

Through prayer God hears us and He answers. It does not always mean "yes," though. Rachel and Hannah waited many years before God opened their wombs even though they prayed regularly. Sometimes God's answer is "no" and sometimes it is simply "not right now." God's timing is perfect and according to His will, not ours.

In Mark 11:24, Jesus says, "Therefore I say to you, whatever things you ask when you pray, believe that you receive them, and you will have them." Solomon wrote that the "the prayer of the upright is His delight" (Proverbs 15:8). Paul wrote in Philippians 4:6, "Be anxious for nothing, but in everything by prayer and supplication, with thanksgiving, let your requests be made known to God." No matter what is on your heart (healing, direction, concern for others, or help with a difficult situation), lift it up to God in prayer with thanksgiving.

Read God's Word
Prayer is important, but it is also important to read God's words in the Bible. There have been many fathers and mothers in the Bible who have also grieved (Mary, Joseph and King David are just a few examples). But there are also stories of grace, healing and forgiveness. Take the time to read the Bible. He specifically wanted these stories in the Bible because they tell us that thousands of years ago other people were experiencing the same events and feelings we are today. Feelings do not change. It hurts when we lose someone we love. God knows this firsthand. Read His word. Read the Bible. There is comfort within those pages.

Cry out to God
In Psalm 34:17-18, David wrote, "The righteous cry out, and the Lord hears and delivers them out of all their troubles. The Lord is near to those who have a broken heart, and saves such as have a contrite spirit." I have cried out to God on many occasions – in prayer in the middle of the night, while writing in my prayer journal, when I am walking, sitting next to Emma's grave and even while weeding the garden. Each and every time I cry out with tears streaming down my face, I feel God's presence. He loves me just as He loves you. John 3:16 says God loved the world so much that He sent His only Son to die on the cross for our sins so that we would not perish but have eternal life. He knows what we feel because His Son died too. He comforts me in my sorrow just as He can comfort you. Open up to Him, cry out to Him. He will hear and console you, wrap His arms around you and cover you in His peace.

Rejoice in today & count your blessings
Jesus said in Matthew 6:34, "Therefore do not worry about tomorrow, for tomorrow will worry about its own things. Sufficient for the day is its own trouble." We can only focus on today, this moment in time.

Finding out I was pregnant completely changed our focus – from saving for land and vacations to paying for the midwife and putting our family goals on hold while we prepared for Emma's arrival. I wondered if I would still be able to quit my job. A short nine months later we were figuring out funeral arrangements, headstone designs and through it all, grieving the loss of our daughter.

The point is, do not worry about tomorrow for we are not guaranteed a minute on this earth. James 4:14 says, "Whereas you do not know what will happen tomorrow. For what is your life? It is even a vapor that appears for a little time and then vanishes away." So rejoice, I say, rejoice! Rejoice in the moment that you're in right now. Start small if necessary, such as taking the next breath or even getting through the next five minutes without tears. I came to realize that every single day is a blessing in and of itself. It's a gift from God.

God turns trials into triumphs

This was one of the messages that Brother Dan delivered during Emma's memorial service. I have been through many trials and tribulations in my life as I am sure you have as well. But when I look back over those difficult times, every trial was turned into a triumph.

Our earthly loss of Emma (a trial) was heaven's gain (a triumph). We witnessed others grow stronger in their relationship with Christ. Johnny and I are now so in tune and part of each other and God that our marriage is stronger than ever. We have a three chord strand between God, Johnny and me. It cannot be broken.

One of my best friends from grade school attended Emma's funeral. I had not seen Amy in over eighteen years but she made the time to come and pay her respects to us and Emma. About three to four weeks after the service Amy sent me an email that she had the words "God Turns Trials Into Triumphs" tattooed on her back in honor of Emma and to remember the strength we can have every single day.

Charlotte, our midwife, told me she hung Emma's picture in her closet. She said she sees it every morning as she gets dressed and remembers she can be strong.

We have strength in our trials and tribulations through God. He gives us what we need when we need it. There is no way that Johnny and I could be where we are now without God giving us the strength He did. As I quoted earlier, Philippians 4:13 says, "I can do all things through Christ who strengthens me." It is not by our doing, but by God's. Through our God-given strength and faith others have come to know Jesus. In 2 Corinthians 2:8-10 Paul is explaining that he had a "thorn in the flesh" and when he prayed to God for deliverance from this "thorn," his answer was:

> *Concerning this thing I pleaded with the Lord three times that it might depart from me. And He said to me, "My grace is sufficient for you, for My strength is made perfect in weakness." Therefore most gladly I will rather boast in my infirmities, that the power of Christ may rest upon me. Therefore I take pleasure in infirmities, in reproaches, in needs, in persecutions, in distresses, for Christ's sake. For when I am weak, then I am strong.*

Every day I thank God for our blessings, trials and tribulations. For it is in my weakness that God gives me strength.

About two months before Emma was born our Tahoe needed repairs. Thank God (I truly mean that) that Johnny knows how to work on cars. It was a rather cold day for Texas. Johnny was having problems with getting the part to fit correctly and had been in and out of the house calling the parts store and trying different tools to get the new part back in. After a few hours I walked outside as it started to rain (so now Johnny's cold, wet and probably very frustrated). He was standing in front of the Tahoe with its hood up and car parts and tools scattered on the ground around him. He looked up at me, smiled, turned his face to the sky, raised his hands and triumphantly hollered toward heaven, "Thank you, Lord, for my trials and tribulations!"

The book of James says, "My brethren, count it all joy when you fall into various trials, knowing that the testing of your faith produces patience" (James 1:2-3). It's through faith that I can say thank you Lord for *all* my trials (including Emma's death).

God has a plan for each of us

Before she was even born God had a plan for Emma, not a plan for her life but one for her death. He knew she was going to die and in knowing that, He gave us the strength we would need to see us through our grieving and to help others in the process. In the book of Jeremiah, God is talking to Jeremiah about his future and his calling. He tells Jeremiah, "Before I formed you in the womb I knew you; before you were born I sanctified you; I ordained you a prophet to the nations" (Jeremiah 1:5). That verse holds true for you and me as well. Emma fulfilled her calling simply by going home to heaven (so through that we would have a testimony of God's love and perfect will in our lives). I still have work to do and a plan from God that needs to be completed. Pay attention for what God's plan is for you and your life.

Our actions create a ripple effect

Our reactions to events create a ripple effect, starting with us and reaching out to first one ring of people (family and close friends), then expanding to the next ring that consists of those we may not have even met (friends of friends) and then on and on until it fans out across the water. This is true not only in this situation, but in everything we do.

Do you realize that people are watching you? They watch everything you do whether you realize it or not and they make judgments about you based on the clothes you wear, your comments, your actions, who you hang around with, or where you go. I did not realize this until the day Emma died. I take that back – probably not until after we returned from the hospital.

As I mentioned before, we had many visitors while we were in the hospital. But for each person that came in, they were embraced in love, not just love from us, but love from God in the form of the Holy Spirit, who moved in and among the people in our room. It was such a tangible love that others could feel it. Despite our loss the peace that filled our room was simply amazing. Brother Dan even commented on how well we were taking Emma's death. We conveyed to him just like everyone we saw that day that we knew Emma was in Jesus' arms and one day we would see her again. We talked about Emma sliding down rainbows and picking flowers in the clouds.

I have not questioned God as to why Emma was called home to heaven. His timing, His will and His plan far supersede anything I could ever imagine or know. I simply have to trust in Him and know that He had a better plan for Emma and for us.

We have not done anything amazing. We have simply planted ourselves in God's garden of grace and love and we are blooming where we are planted. People often ask how we are able to do what we do and continue on with our lives. Believe me - we miss Emma every single day. She is always in our thoughts and hearts. Yes, it is difficult. Yes, we still grieve. And yes, I still know it is for the best because it is according to God's plan.

By our actions others see that we're living our faith daily, minute by minute. They are watching us, just as they are watching you in whatever battle you are facing. As I said before, it is not by our own strength. If that were the case we would be cynical, negative people living in a deep pit of despair and blackness. But instead God has given us the strength that we need to make it through our loss. It is only by His grace, mercy and love that we can continue as we do. We stand on the solid rock of Jesus.

I do not think I will ever fully know how far-reaching our life-ripples extend, not just to those we know, but to those we have never even met. My hope is that through our loss we will be able to plant seeds for God so that others can bloom where they are planted in God's beautiful garden.

It's okay to laugh and cry (at the same time)

Emotions are simply that – emotions. They can roll through us like a thunderstorm blowing across the Texas Hill Country – fast and furious with tornado-type winds or slow and steady drowning us in a flood of tears. Either way, let them come.

I tried to read a devotional book on grieving but stopped a few days into it. I found that I cried in anguish with every devotional. It really did not help my overall outlook on Emma's passing. I have never grieved like this before. Yes, I miscarried 13 years ago when I was seven weeks pregnant but I carried Emma for nine months only to lose her at the very end.

I laughed and cried and finally realized that I was not losing my mind. I was being human – just as God made me to be. He made us to *feel* our emotions, plain and simple. Life is not always a bed of roses (if it were I would not be writing this book). He made us to laugh and cry, dance and mourn (just as it states in Ecclesiastes 3). Do not fear or hide from what the Lord has given you – emotions of grief, love, laughter, sorrow, heartache, joy, anger, etc. It is through these emotions that we heal.

Grieving is a process and can take many forms. There is not a specific right or wrong way to grieve - so laugh or cry or do both at the same time. Grieve your child's death but please understand that while she is dead here on earth she is alive in heaven!

The Little Things Matter

Right after losing Emma, it was not discussing Emma or her death that caused me the most grief. It was the little reminders of her absence that hurt: seeing her empty bed, the folded clothes and her blankets. It was my milk coming in and the painful engorgement, the reminder that I did not have a baby to feed. It was the longing in my heart to hold her close to me. It was the quiet nights and the tiny socks I found under the bed two months later. It was Emma's car seat sitting in the corner or all the bottles in the cabinet. The little things are what hurt the most for they were the reminders of what was not to be.

Over the course of a few weeks I slowly started to remove those little reminders. I gave away the stroller, bottles, extra diapers, baby hangers, bibs, and most everything else. I boxed up her clothes and put them in the shed. I wrapped her car seat in huge trash bags and placed it in the shed as well, eventually giving it away to a single mother who was expecting her first child. Every time I gave an item away, the pain eased. And for every item I gave away, I told Emma's story, of God's love for them and His plan for Emma. It was like letting her go, a little at a time, but at the same time, spreading God's love. While I still trusted Jesus and God's plan, the pain was still there. When I took Emma's crib apart, I cried out to God and kneeled in prayer every few minutes.

If it helps, snuggle with something of your child's at night. I snuggled with Emma's polka-dotted baby blanket as it was the only tangible thing we had from the hospital that wrapped her. I found it comforting to hold something that once held her. Even now I will pull it out and wrap up in it, cherishing those few special memories I have of holding her.

But now I look forward to the little things. In the morning I thank God for the gift of another day. I look forward to spending time with James and Lauren, making Johnny's coffee, writing and reading God's Word. I enjoy watering Emma's tree at the cemetery – knowing that in the spring it will be a beautiful display of white flowers. I pull out Emma's things every now and then – all the little outfits my friends from the office decorated, her memorial box from the hospital, her pictures, her locket of hair, even her little photo album. These little mementos of Emma are all that I have left and I cherish them. The little things do matter, in everything.

You are still a Mom (or Dad)

If you lost your one and only child through stillbirth or some other way, you are still a parent. Don't you dare think otherwise.

For the moms of deceased infants, you carried that precious baby for nine months. You went through morning sickness, aches, pains, heartburn, kicks and hiccups (not to mention those who suffered through gestational diabetes or pre-eclampsia). You delivered your sweet baby into this world and your baby is still with you in your heart.

For the fathers, you were with your wife throughout the whole experience – from the morning sickness to putting the crib together and installing the car seat. You worried over your wife and baby and attended the doctor appointments and saw your beautiful baby in the sonogram. You heard your child's heartbeat and felt him kick your hand when you touched your wife's belly. Perhaps you even put your head next to your child and spoke or sang a song to him. Your son or daughter is still part of your family. Simply because your child is buried does not mean he or she never existed.

Emma's pictures are displayed on a shelf right next to James' and Lauren's. We visit her grave as a family to water her crepe myrtle tree. James and Lauren helped decide what to put on Emma's headstone. We are all part of this family and our children know that. Your child lives in heaven and if you have accepted Jesus as your Lord and Savior, you'll meet him there one day. Death may separate you now, but the Bible says as believers in Jesus Christ we will join our babies in heaven. Rejoice in that!!!

It's OK to talk about death

I was amazed at the number of women who have approached me saying they also had a miscarriage, stillbirth or some other pregnancy complication. According to the American Pregnancy Association[6], there are approximately six million pregnancies in America each year. Of that six million, a little over four million are live births and almost two million account for pregnancy losses (approximately thirty-seven percent). Of the two million losses:

- 600,000 miscarry
- 1,200,000 terminate the pregnancy
- 64,000 have ectopic pregnancies
- 6,000 have molar pregnancies
- 26,000 have stillbirths

Let's break that down again. One in three American families experiences the loss of a child. Aside from terminated pregnancies there are approximately 700,000 pregnancy losses a year. Ninety percent of that 700,000 are due to stillbirths and miscarriages.

I don't want to completely leave out the terminated pregnancies for they account for sixty-three percent of all pregnancy losses in a

---

[6] http://www.americanpregnancy.org/main/statistics.html

year. The loss of a child is the loss of a child regardless of how it happens. Those sweet babies are now in heaven and their mothers are still affected by the loss of their little ones in some way.

Even though one-third of all pregnancy losses reflect the parents themselves, it is still a small fraction of how many people are impacted from the loss of one baby - other children, grandparents, aunts and uncles.

Through our own loss, I have learned that it is completely okay to talk about death and heaven and everything in between regarding Emma. I am really okay with it. I may cry or I may smile with a radiant joy. Regardless, I want to talk about my sweet little baby. I *want* people to understand God had a purpose and a plan for her life. Maybe you're not ready and that is okay, too, but just know that you are not alone.

Stay busy (but find time each day to be still).

If it helps, find a new hobby or pick up an old one. It helped me in the early days following Emma's death to keep my mind and hands busy. I did lots of reading, baking, quilting, gardening and spending time with James and Lauren. Then, there were times that I would simply be still, rest and listen to God.

Talk (Or Write) It Out

Talk to someone who has been where you are. God has put people in my life who understand what I am going through. They have a wealth of wisdom to offer and can often provide needed support simply because they have walked the path I am on. Surround yourself with friends and family, people who love you and will support you emotionally and spiritually. It has helped us so much to have fellow Christians love and pray for us. They really helped us to get through.

If you do not have anyone you can talk to or feel comfortable talking with, try writing down your thoughts and feelings. This has also helped. I wrote during my pregnancy so it was only natural for me to continue writing after Emma's death. It helped me express my feelings in a way that sometimes I could not express verbally. Try writing as a way of releasing and living through your grief. It may help you as well.

Chapter 7
Shine On

Let your light so shine before men, that they may see your good works and glorify your Father in heaven. – Matthew 5:16

Do you know how many passages in the Bible relate to light? According to the website www.twopaths.com[7] the King James Bible has the word "light" written 272 times. Here are just a few:

- *The Lord is my light and my salvation, whom shall I fear? The Lord is the strength of my life; of whom shall I be afraid?* - Psalm 27:1
- *Your word is a lamp to my feet and a light to my path.* - Psalm 119:105
- *The light of the righteous rejoices, but the lamp of the wicked will be put out.* - Proverbs 13:9
- *Truly the light is sweet, and it is pleasant for the eyes to behold the sun.* - Ecclesiastes 11:7
- *O House of Jacob, come and let us walk in the light of the Lord.* - Isaiah 2:5
- *You are the light of the world. A city that is set on a hill cannot be hidden. Nor do they light a lamp and put it under a basket, but on a lampstand, and it gives light to all who are in the house. Let your light so shine before men, that they may see your good works and glorify your Father in heaven.* - Matthew 5:14-16
- *In Him was life, and the life was the light of men.* - John 1:4
- *For you were once darkness, but now you are light in the Lord. Walk as children of light...* - Ephesians 5:8

There are many other passages, but from these few, we can understand that God intended light to be good. Even in Genesis, at the very creation of the world, God created light on the first day. And, in Revelation 21:23, John describes the new heaven and earth

---

[7] http://www.twopaths.com/faq_WordCount.htm

and the new Holy City, the New Jerusalem. This city "had no need of the sun or of the moon to shine in it, for the glory of God illuminated it. The Lamb is its light." From the beginning God created light in the sun and the moon but in the new beginning, He will be the light.

As followers of Christ we need to be the light of Jesus until He returns. Through us and our light, others may come to know Jesus and want to be part of what we have in Jesus' family.

It is not always easy to be the light. When you are in your darkest hour and you feel as if there is no hope or light that is when your light needs to shine the brightest. Your internal light does not come from you. It comes from Jesus, from the faith you have in Him that all will be well. If I did not love Jesus or have the faith foundation that I do, it would have been so easy to fall into black despair. In the months since Emma's death, I have often wondered how differently life would be if my faith was weak or even if I had no faith. I would have no hope, no joy, no promise of what is yet to come. It would be an angry, bitter existence, blaming God for Emma's death.

There comes a time in our lives when we must walk the walk of a Christian instead of just paying lip service to a religion. We cannot praise God for the good and blame Him for the bad. He took an unfortunate situation and used it as a way to bring others to Him. Yes, God is ultimately in control of everything on earth. But, life happens. We can either choose to put our faith in God and walk the walk, living as Christians every single day or we can blame God Monday through Saturday and live as Christians only on Sunday. That is not a relationship with Christ. Being a Christian means you have a one-on-one relationship with your Lord and Savior, Jesus Christ. When you are in the trenches and dealing with a horrible situation, you walk on faith that God will take care of you and lead you through it. He offers you His hand every single day. You can either choose to take it and let Him lead you through the fire, or you can try to make it alone. Turning our backs on God during this point of our lives was not an option for us.

I took a leap of faith months before Emma was born and quit my job not knowing how our finances would turn out but knowing that God would provide. He called me to be home full time - to be the caretaker of my home and family. At the time we had money in savings and were debt free. My faith was really tested after Emma was stillborn and we had new medical bills to pay. Our income was cut in half and then became almost non-existent after Johnny was let go, not even three months after Emma's death. Yet even today we are still relying on God to provide opportunities for Johnny through his real estate business.

My hope and faith is in Jesus Christ. My prayers are always answered, but not always the way I want them answered. As the saying goes, I have learned that I simply need to let go and let God.

The worldview focuses on humans controlling their lives, being the makers of their own destinies. However, do you not think that the Maker of the Universe is capable of being in control of my humble little life? It is okay to not be in control. The times I thought I was in control I was acting outside of God's will and those have been the times when I have been the farthest from Him. I didn't put my trust in Him. I thought I could handle it better but that was simply an illusion. That is when my world would fall apart. But, by turning situations, people, or events over to God, I have seen miracles happen. Doors opened that were closed and other doors closed that had once been open. My trust in God is a solid foundation, not shifting sand. He will lift me up as He provides daily for me and my family.

Saved Through Salvation

Do you know the story of Jonah? God instructed Jonah to go to Nineveh to tell them to turn from their wicked ways. Jonah had no desire to go to Ninevah, so he boarded a ship for Tarshish. God knew what Jonah was doing so He sent a huge storm, so large in fact that the hardened sailors on board were scared. They each cried out to their own god. Jonah was sound asleep below deck, oblivious to all the confusion and chaos of the storm. As the story progresses, the sailors eventually threw Jonah overboard and as soon as they did, the "sea ceased from its raging" (Jonah 1:15). That's when the "great fish" swallowed Jonah and he stayed in the fish's belly for three days and three nights (Jonah 1:17).

During His time in isolation, Jonah did what we should all do, he prayed (Jonah 2:2-9):

> *Out of the belly of Sheol I cried, and You heard my voice. For You cast me into the deep, into the heart of the seas, And the floods surrounded me; all Your billows and Your waves passed over me. Then I said, 'I have been cast out of Your sight; Yet I will look again toward Your holy temple.' The waters surrounded me, even to my soul; The deep closed around me;*

> weeds were wrapped around my head. I went down to the moorings of the mountains; the earth with its bars closed behind me forever; yet You have brought up my life from the pit, O Lord, my God. When my soul fainted within me, I remembered the Lord; and my prayer went up to You, into Your holy temple. Those who regard worthless idols forsake their own mercy. But I will sacrifice to You with the voice of thanksgiving; I will pay what I have vowed. salvation is of the Lord.

In his despair and believing that He was going to die, Jonah knew that God was his only salvation. He gave up his own sinful life (avoiding God, trying to hide in the boat and running away) in order to have God's grace and mercy.

There are two things that really speak to me in these paragraphs in dealing with grief:

1. In his darkest distress Jonah called on God for help. When he was literally drowning in the raging sea and the seaweed was wrapping around his head and pulling him under, when he felt the earth locking him inside its walls of water, he called out to God. When I am in the deepest despair and sorrow over Emma, I call out to God and He hears me.
2. God saved Jonah and lifted him out of the pit of death – not because of anything Jonah did, but because of God's grace alone. God saves me each and every time I think I am drowning in my sorrow.

How many times do we ignore or simply run away from God? By fleeing from God, we are turning away from the grace that could be ours. That grace is what gives us the peace to make it through the grieving process. In the Old Testament, God had a covenant with His people and sins were atoned for through a sacrificial offering (like a lamb), but all that changed with the birth of Jesus (who became the sacrificial lamb for everyone when He died on the cross for our sins).

Do you know what salvation truly is? Webster dictionary defines salvation as a deliverance from the power and effects of sin.

According to Jesus in John 14:6, "I am the way and the truth and the life. No one comes to the Father except through me." Paul states in Acts 4:12, "Salvation is found in no one else, for there is no other name under heaven given to men by which we must be saved." Paul is saying that only in Jesus do we have salvation.

How are we delivered from sin? Sin separates us from God. Jesus bridged the gap between our sin and God's salvation. *How?* He died on the cross for our sins. The only way to receive God's salvation now is through a relationship with Jesus, His Son.

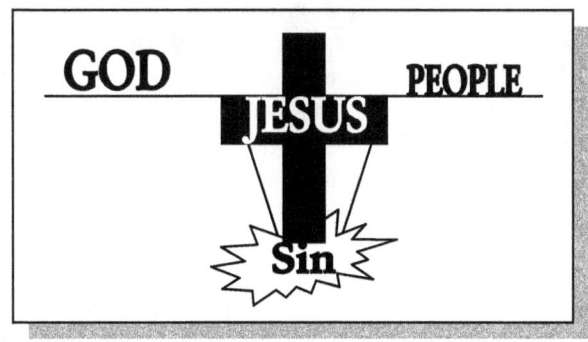

Where do you stand in your relationship with Jesus? Is it built on rock or sand? Are you calling out to Him in your time of grief, in your pit of despair? Please do not hesitate on this. Had Jonah not reached out to God, He probably would not have been saved. Had Jesus not died on the cross for our sins, we would not be saved either – for by His wounds we are healed (1 Peter 2:24).

We are still grieving Emma. It comes to us in waves. Two months had passed after Emma's death and I was doing pretty well. I thought all the bills had come in from our hospital stay and felt that we were on our way back to some normalcy (our new normal that is). But, as I was checking the mail one day there was the bill from the anesthesiologist. Did I want yet another medical bill, another reminder that instead of holding Emma I was holding a statement that said I owed money due to her death? I wanted to curl into a ball and cry. But I realized in the scheme of things that this is just a bill. It does not determine my salvation.

I stood firm on God's Word and the promise of eternal life that Jesus fulfilled on the cross. Through God's grace I have salvation. I know that despite these physical reminders that Emma is not coming back, I will be going to see her one day. Through Jesus, salvation is mine. All I have to do is accept Him as my Lord and Savior and repent of my sins. The same promise holds true for you too.

As a public testament of my faith, I was baptized through immersion at our church, Crestview Baptist Church, on May 15, 2011, two months after Emma died. As I mentioned earlier, I have always known and loved Jesus. I have leaned on Him throughout my life in both the good and bad times. Although my faith journey continues to this day, I wanted to publicly show my commitment and love for Him, a renewal of my love and devotion to Him. Without a doubt, despite our rough financial times and losing Emma, I love Jesus more than ever. My faith has grown stronger in the last few months, during these times of grief. I was baptized as an infant, but as an adult I made the decision to proclaim my faith to all.

God wants you to come to Him. Your salvation is near and is yours for the taking. God is offering it; are you willing to accept the call and take His hand? Are you willing to get out of the boat and walk on the water with Jesus just as Peter did?

Listen to your heavenly Father. Open yourself up to what He wants for you. Let your light shine. Through those dark days of grief, despair or loneliness, you still have hope. That hope is Jesus Christ. He can brighten the darkest spots in your heart and illuminate them for His glory. In doing so, He illuminates you. His word is a lamp to your feet and a light to your path (Psalm 119:105). Read it, devour it, see the light that He holds for you, so that you may know where you are going and how to get there. It will warm your heart and lead you out of the darkness and in doing so you let your light shine as a beacon for others to come out of their own darkness as they seek a relationship with Christ.

Grieve. Grieve for your precious child, your gift from God. But in doing so, continue to let your light shine. Be a beacon of hope for others in their own turmoil and grief. There is light at the end of the tunnel. His name is Jesus Christ. Know Him. Love Him. Trust Him and shine on through your grief.

Chapter 8
A Dad's Perspective

Come now, you who say, "Today or tomorrow we will go to such and such a city, spend a year there, buy and sell, and make a profit"; whereas you do not know what will happen tomorrow. For what is your life? It is even a vapor that appears for a little time and then vanishes away. Instead you ought to say, "If the Lord wills, we shall live and do this or that." – James 4:13-15

While Meredith was still in the hospital, I was walking between two of the hospital buildings and the wind picked up and brushed over me. I stopped in my tracks for it felt as if God had breathed on me and time stood still. I can still remember the feelings of the wind and the sunshine, seeing the crepe myrtles, and the crazy thing is I realized with clarity that all is God's, was God's and will be God's.

The book of James clearly states that life is just a mist (James 4:13-15). We are not promised one day on this earth. In realizing this I understood just what Jesus' brother, James, was saying. It is almost as if all the moments leading to this point all came to a super pinpoint conclusion. I realized that all my plans were meaningless and that God is the master of time, events, life and death. We may plan our path, but the Lord chooses our footsteps on that path (Proverbs 16:9).

When you bring life down to just this, you then realize that God is maturing us, building us, and loving us through tragedies and tribulations. Again, James mentions we begin to gain strength, perseverance, faith, and finally hope in all things. Tragedies are not always a form of punishment. They may simply be a form of God molding us like clay to the person He wants us to be. We can then go to the world and share our testimony to others and witness to them. We can be a light in a dark world.

James warns us about planning our lives. Who are we to even think for a minute we have that much power? In the same breath he basically states that it is wrong to boast of anything futuristic regarding our own lives and warns us to focus on today, the moment,

Through Keller Williams, we received a grant that paid for all of our hospital expenses and they even purchased Emma's headstone. On a cold day in late January 2012, ten months after Emma's death, we installed her headstone.

Around this time, Johnny was asked by Keller Williams co-founder, Mary Tennant, if she could use his story as part of her inspirational message at the national Keller Williams Family Reunion convention. By God's grace again, the door opened for Johnny to travel to Orlando, Florida to hear this speech and to attend as a guest of honor when Ms. Tennant spoke to the 8,500 agents present. Emma's story was told yet again with the recurring theme to let your light shine.

Do you see the pattern? Through God's grace, Emma's story has been told repeatedly for the past year. It is not for our glory or even for Emma's glory, but for God's. Yes, our sweet little girl went home to heaven before she even took her first breath. But the heartwarming part is that our daughter's death has touched so many people, all for the glory of God's kingdom. That is a true honor for us. Our purpose since losing Emma has been to not only tell her story, but Jesus' story of love, grace, forgiveness and mercy, even in the face of grief.

I won't lie to you. I still grieve Emma, but it's not a despairing type of grief, rather a longing in my heart to hold my baby. I miss her every single day and think of her often. For now I simply wait for the time God calls me home to heaven. In the meantime, we serve Him by telling Emma's story, of our miracle baby that fulfilled her God-given plan simply by going to heaven. Through her death our testimony has grown. We are honored to do so, honored to let our light shine so that others may come to know Jesus.

www.ingramcontent.com/pod-product-compliance
Lightning Source LLC
Chambersburg PA
CBHW071314040426
42444CB00009B/2011